M. C. ESCHER™
Daybook & Journal

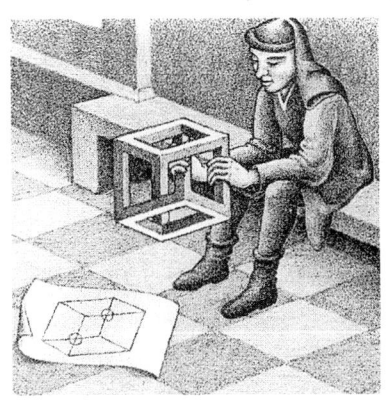

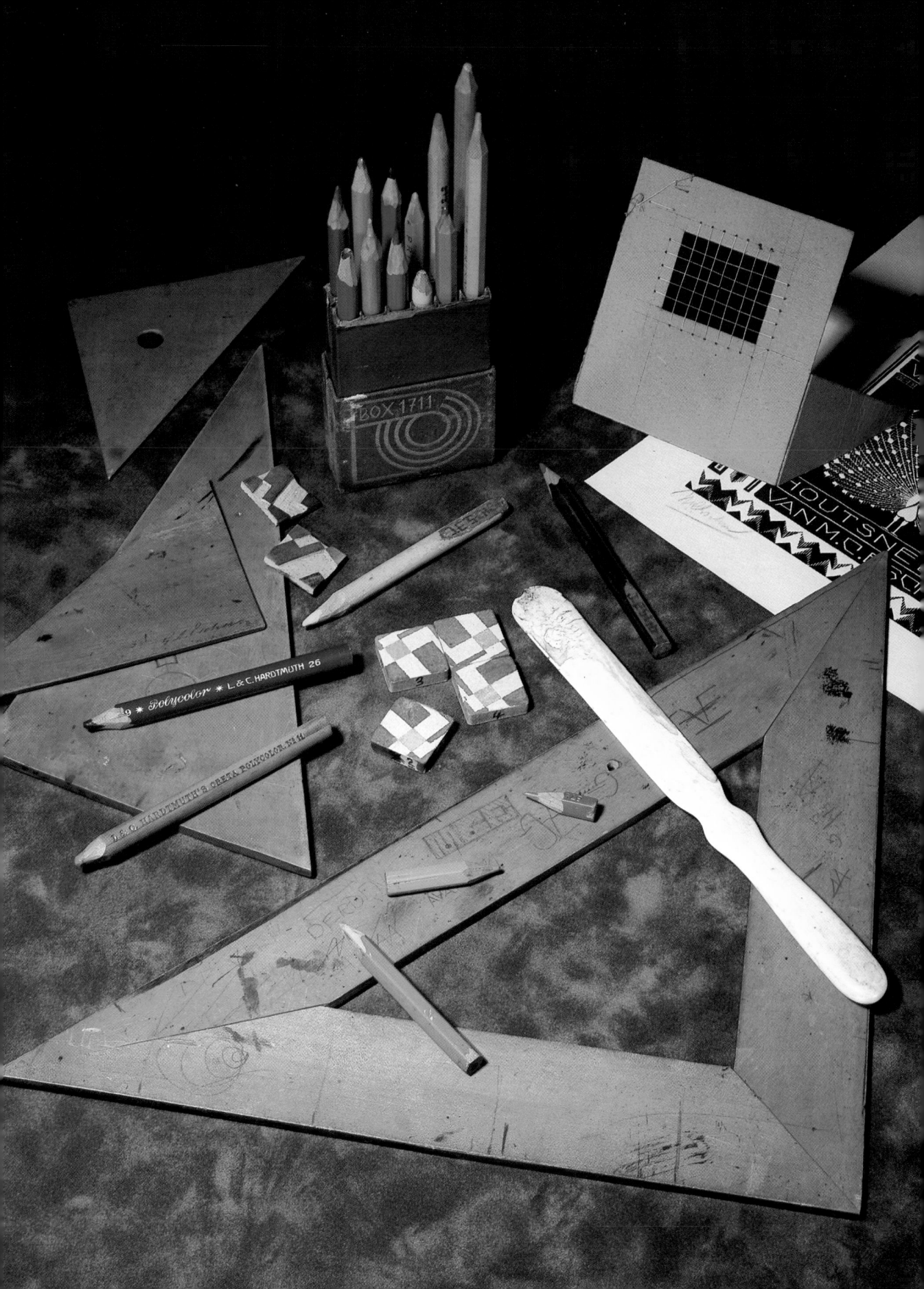

M. C. ESCHER™

Daybook & Journal

Compiled by Bruno Ernst

POMEGRANATE ARTBOOKS · SAN FRANCISCO

Credits:

The Escher prints were obtained
from the archives of the M. C.
Escher Foundation/Cordon Art,
Baarn, Holland.

The photographs and illustrations
on pages 6, 8, 36, 40, 42, 54, 57, 67,
78, 80, 83, 84, 88, 94, 98, 100, 103,
104 and 109 are by J. A. F. de Rijk
(Bruno Ernst).

The illustration reproduced on
pages 2 and 120 is from the Artists'
Market Collection.

The photograph on page 74 is
courtesy of Oscar Reutersvärd.

The designs reproduced on page 51
are from the museum of Joh.
Enschedé & Zn.

Graphic layout: Pieter van Delft,
ADM International bv, Amsterdam
Typesetting and lithography: Boxem
bv, Amsterdam
English translation: The Wordmill,
Healdsburg, California
First printing of English edition:
March 1995

Printed in Spain

© 1995 Bookman International bv,
Houtweg 11, 1251 CR Laren, The
Netherlands
Compilation, text and photographic
material © 1995 J. A. F. de Rijk
All M.C. Escher prints © 1995 M. C.
Escher Foundation/Cordon Art,
Baarn, Holland, phone
+31.2154.18041, fax
+31.2154.11766.
All rights reserved.

Published by Pomegranate Artbooks
Box 6099
Rohnert Park, CA 94927

Pomegranate Europe Ltd.
Fullbridge House, Fullbridge
Maldon, Essex CM9 7LE
England

ISBN 0-87654-106-6

Introduction

Maurits Cornelis ESCHER is world famous and as much a part of the Netherlands as windmills, tulips, Rembrandt and van Gogh. Since he was born at the end of the previous century, in 1898, and lived until 1972, he was a contemporary for many of us. The son of an engineer, Escher was born in Leeuwarden, the capital of the province of Friesland. He took the final exam for graduation from high school at the age of twenty and failed it. In 1919, after a brief attempt to study architecture at the prestigious engineering school in Delft, he enrolled in the School for Architectural and Decorative Arts in Haarlem.

There he soon abandoned the idea of studying architecture and instead began to study drawing from nature and the technique of producing woodcuts. He trained in particular under the Dutch artist Jessurun de Mesquita. Upon completion of the school's curriculum, which took barely two years, he left school and embarked on a period of traveling and drawing. In Italy, he met and married Jetta Umiker. The couple took up residence in Rome, where Escher lived and worked until 1935. He became the father of three sons, George, Arthur and Jan. After living for a short time in Switzerland and Belgium, Escher settled in the Netherlands, where he lived in the town of Baarn until two years before his death. His last two years were spent in the Rosa Spier Home, a retirement home with nursing care for elderly artists, in the town of Laren.

Until his departure from Rome at age thirty-seven, Escher led an extremely varied life. But the work he produced during these years was hardly distinguishable from that of other Dutch graphic artists of the period. He certainly was not the best or the most well known among them. When we talk about an "Escher print" today, we convey a specific meaning that could be described as "a print from the period after 1935." The expression "Escherian" also refers to characteristics of Escher's later prints.

Escher's most productive period began when he was about forty years old. By then, he appeared to be leading a tranquil life. He lived somewhat secludedly in Baarn, traveled occasionally, exhibited and gave lectures about his work.

He continued to take a keen interest in his children's lives as they grew into adulthood. He kept them informed of everyday events in his life, and he sometimes wrote about the prints on which he was working. He became well known and recognized, especially by scholars in the area of the exact sciences. Twice he was even proposed as a candidate for an

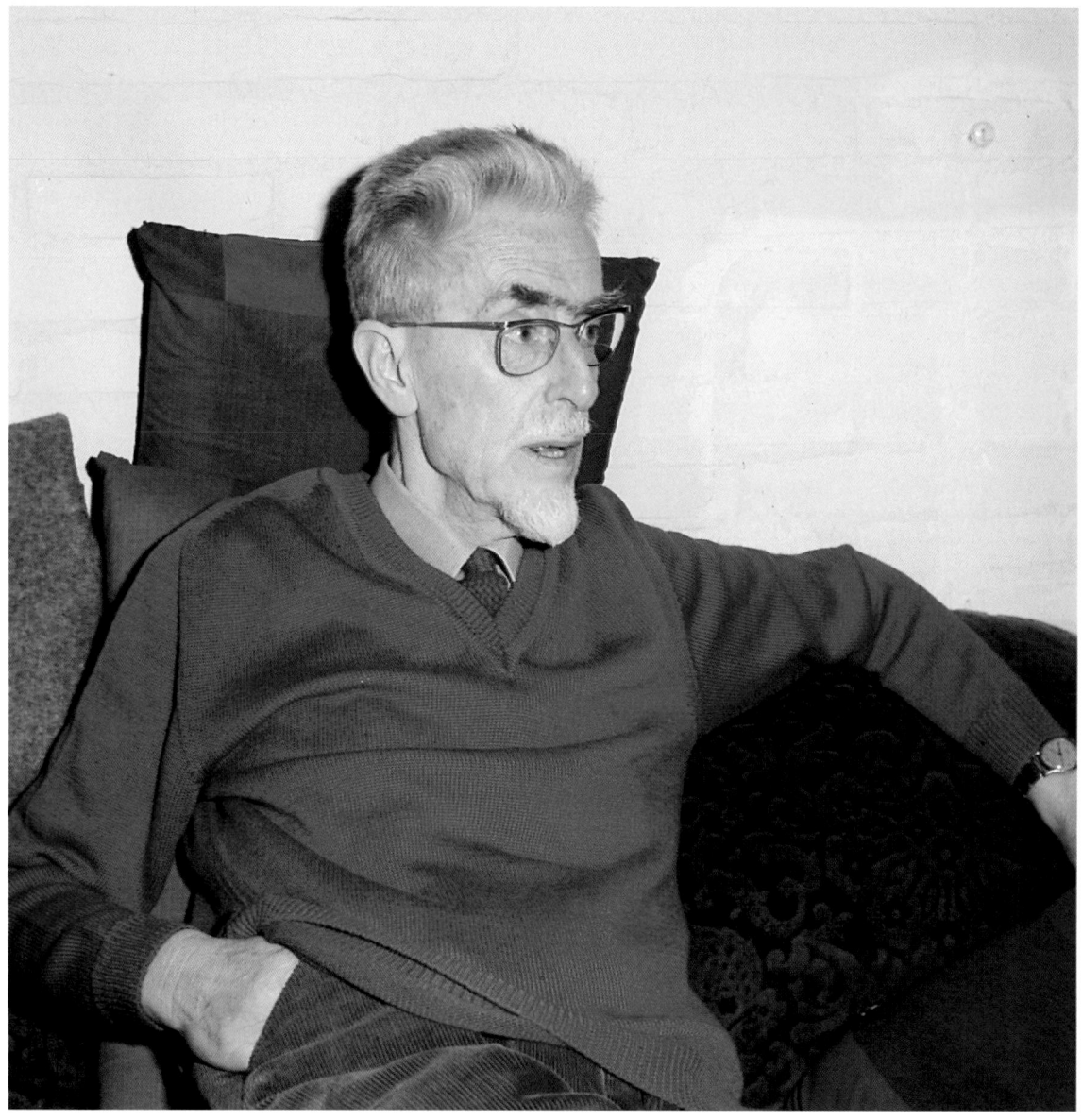

Portrait of Escher

Drawing Hands
Lithograph, 1948

Can a hand draw a hand? Of course it can!

But can the hand in the drawing draw yet another hand? This is the intriguing problem depicted by Escher in this lithograph. Although the answer to the question is, of course, that it cannot be done, it is impossible to make out in the drawing which hand is the "real" one. The theme here is that drawing is deceiving!

This leads to some very interesting speculation. For example, can we build a machine that can build itself? In biology, this is an accepted concept, but can we use our modern technology to construct machines that recreate themselves? Or can a system, such as Euclidean geometry, prove itself? There is a link here between Escher and the mathematician and logician Kurt Gödel.

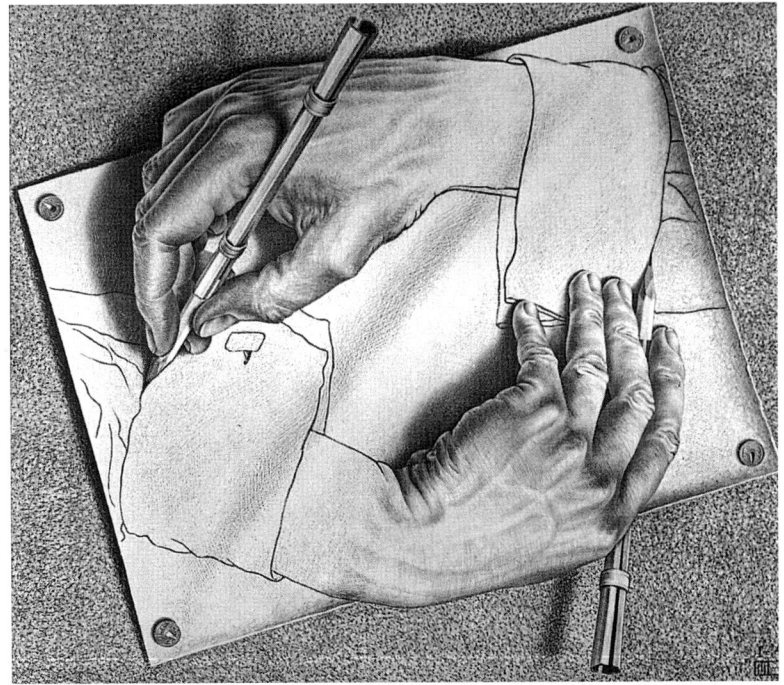

honorable doctorate at a university in the Netherlands, although he himself never knew about it.

All in all, Escher's life did not provide the substance for an exciting tale—but his prints do. They tell the story of the discovery of a new world. That is why the story of how his prints originated is the main focus of this journal. In recounting the tale, I will follow the chronological events of his life to the extent possible.

Escher's prints constitute a cohesive body of work. Every one of them is fascinating in that it portrays one of Escher's discoveries. But these discoveries were not isolated events. Escher did not randomly look for interesting concepts that would astound the viewer. The important element of his work after 1935 is precisely that he researched very specific subjects that intrigued him and then captured each new discovery that surprised and astonished him in a print, for the purpose of communicating to others his enthusiasm about these new discoveries. As an introduction to the story of Escher's life, this journal presents a summary of the subjects he explored and illustrates them with a number of his prints.

Bruno Ernst, Utrecht, August 1993

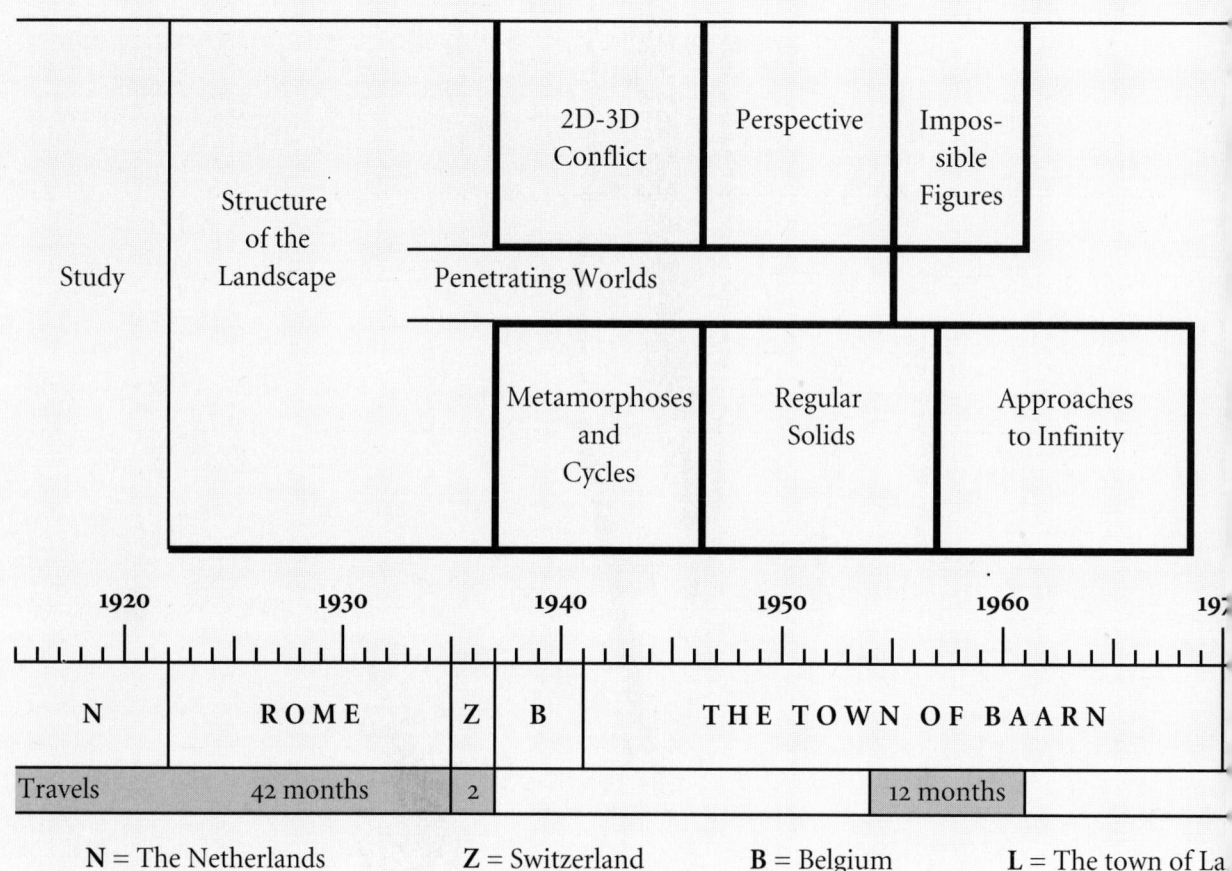

			2D-3D Conflict	Perspective	Impos- sible Figures	
Study	Structure of the Landscape	Penetrating Worlds				
			Metamorphoses and Cycles	Regular Solids	Approaches to Infinity	

1920	1930	1940	1950	1960	197
N	ROME	Z B	THE TOWN OF BAARN		

Travels   42 months   2   12 months

N = The Netherlands   **Z** = Switzerland   **B** = Belgium   **L** = The town of La

**Graphic Representation of
Escher's Life and Work**

Before his fortieth year, Escher produced hardly any "Escher prints," for which the explanation is as follows. Until 1938, Escher's work did not show a clear trend. He had produced mainly prints of landscapes, had become somewhat well known as a result of his exhibitions and was appreciated as a competent graphic artist. After 1938, his philosophical bent began to be revealed in his work. He set out to study problems in three areas: the structure of space, the structure of plane and the relationship between space and plane when depicting space. Each discovery Escher made in these areas was recorded in a print, not as a sober statement but as an expression of wonder and enthusiasm. It was this quality of his work that gained him a worldwide following for his abstract ideas. When one analyzes his prints, it becomes clear that there is a relationship among them: each print originates from a previous one. There is little repetition in his work. He always worked on several themes at the same time as well. This can be seen from the flowchart presented above.

Beneath the time line, Escher's places of residence are shown as well as the number of months during which he traveled for extended periods of time. Above the time line, the themes are indicated with which Escher dealt successively and simultaneously. In the following pages, we will discuss each of these themes as portrayed in a print. We will then go on to take a look at Escher's life in a more chronological order.

1

       ★

2

       ★

3

       ★

4

       ★

5

       ★

6

       ★

7

       ★

Castrovalva
Lithograph, 1930

The Structure of Space:
Landscape Prints
Even in Escher's early landscape prints, we can detect his tendency to give structure to space. In the lithograph ***Castrovalva*** (a small town in the Abruzzi mountains of Italy), the emphasis is more on filling up the area of the drawing three-dimensionally than on its composition. "I still remember that while I was sketching this landscape, I heard children singing in a school somewhere above me to the left," Escher later told me.

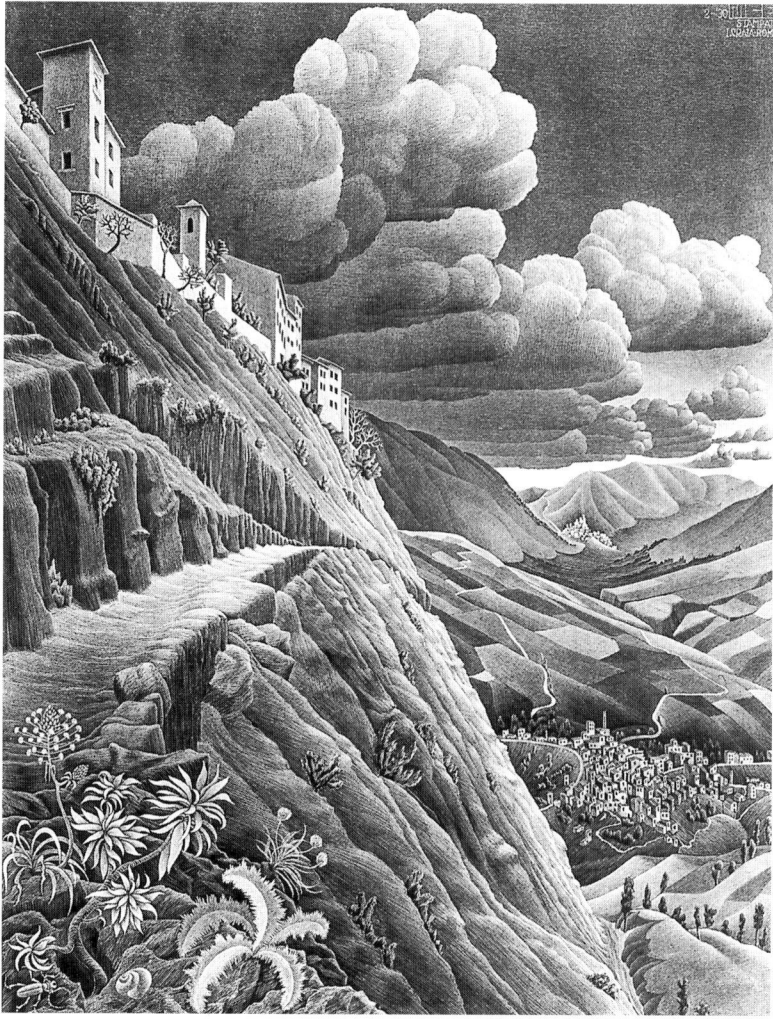

8

★

9

★

10

★

11

★

12

★

13

★

14

★

Hand with Reflecting Sphere
Lithograph, 1935

The Structure of Space:
Penetrating Worlds
Can space be occupied more than
once by matter or, more simply
put, can two worlds take up the
same space at the same time? One
possible way would be through
reflection. In **Hand with
Reflecting Sphere**, a lithograph
produced in 1935, we see Escher's
hand holding a spherical mirror.
But at the same time his hand
holds himself and his studio in the
Monte Verde district in Rome.

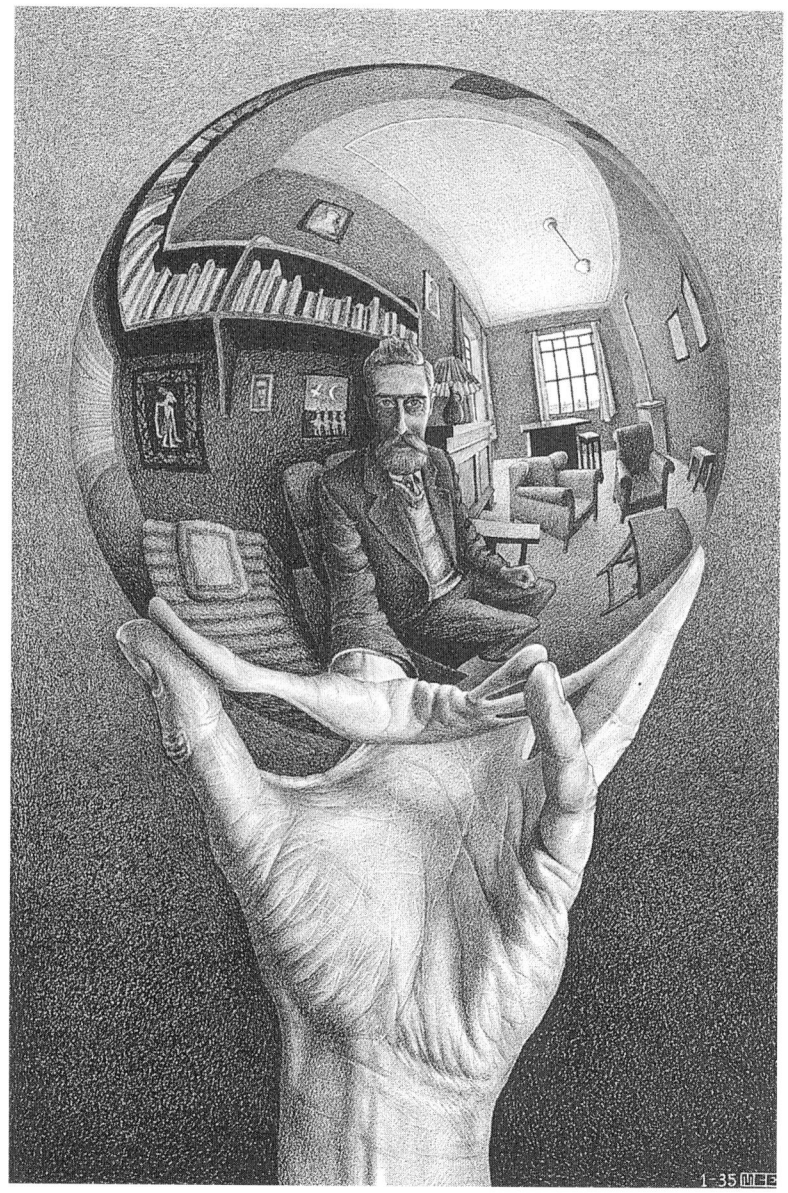

15   ★

16   ★

17   ★

18   ★

19   ★

20   ★

21   ★

22 ★

23 ★

24 ★

25 ★

26 ★

27 ★

28 ★

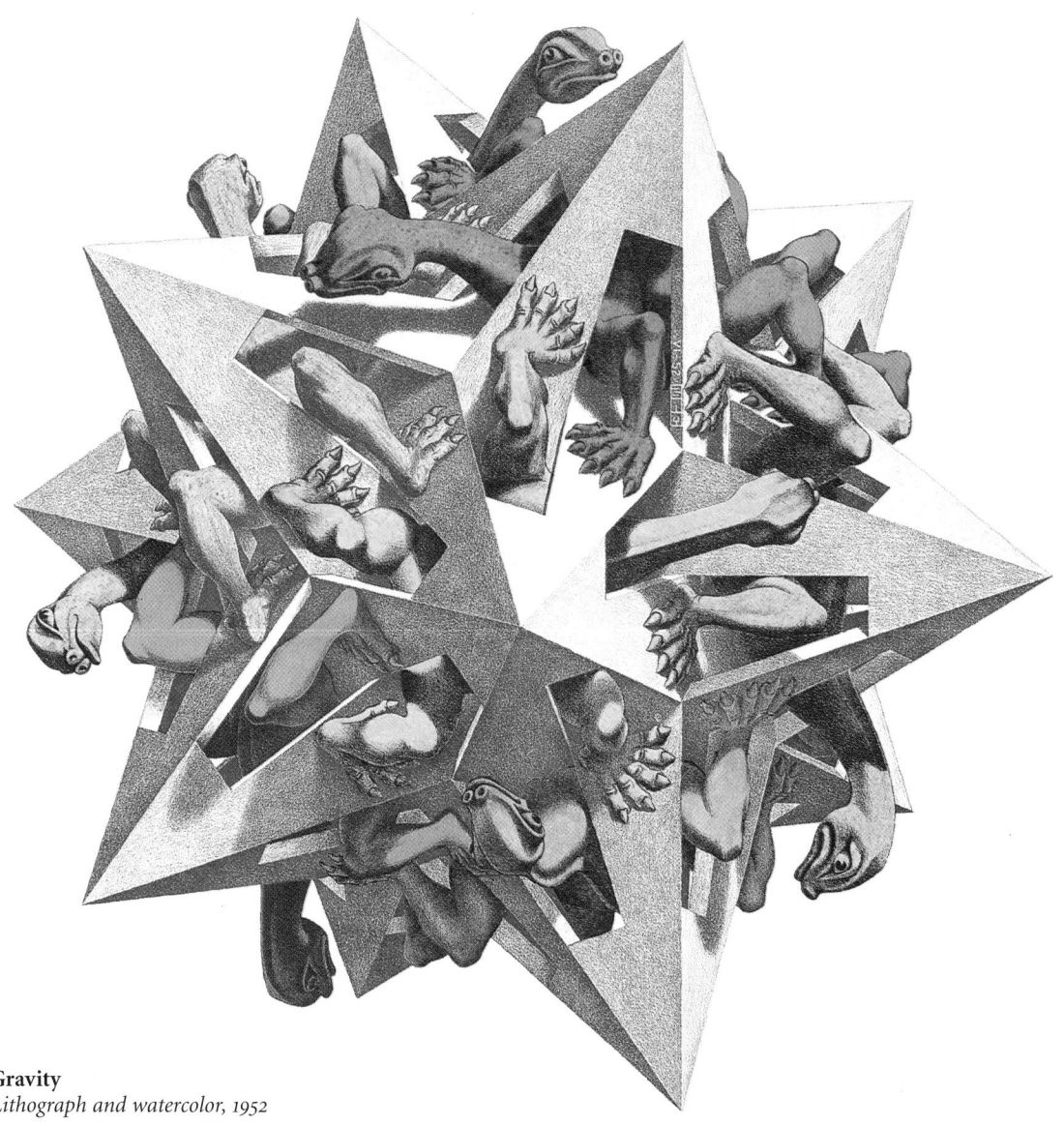

Gravity
Lithograph and watercolor, 1952

The Structure of Space:
Abstract Mathematical Solids
Escher was immensely fascinated
by crystals and by the many other
regular solids invented by
mathematicians. He thoroughly
explored their structures and
interrelationships. ***Gravity***, a
lithograph in colors he created in
1952, is a so-called stellated
dodecahedron, a figure first
described by the German
astronomer Johannes Kepler. A

five-sided pyramid has been drawn
on each of the twelve pentagons.
These pyramids have been opened
up by Escher in order to show
twelve reptiles that are being
pulled toward the inside by the
gravity of their little planets.

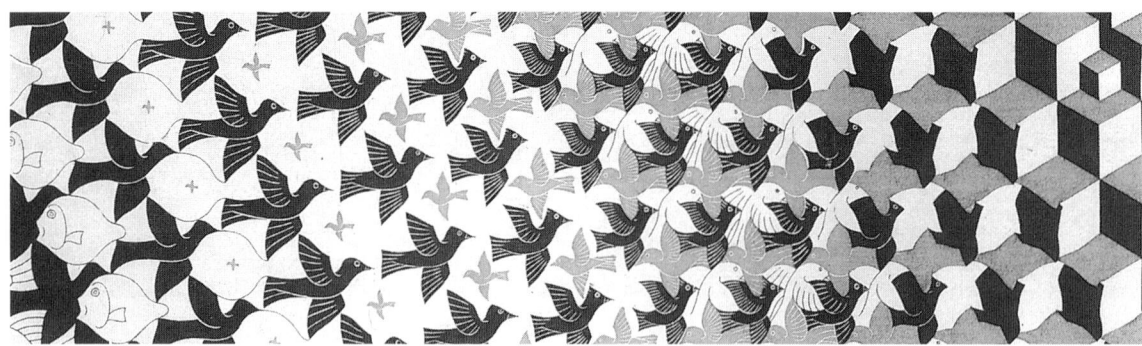

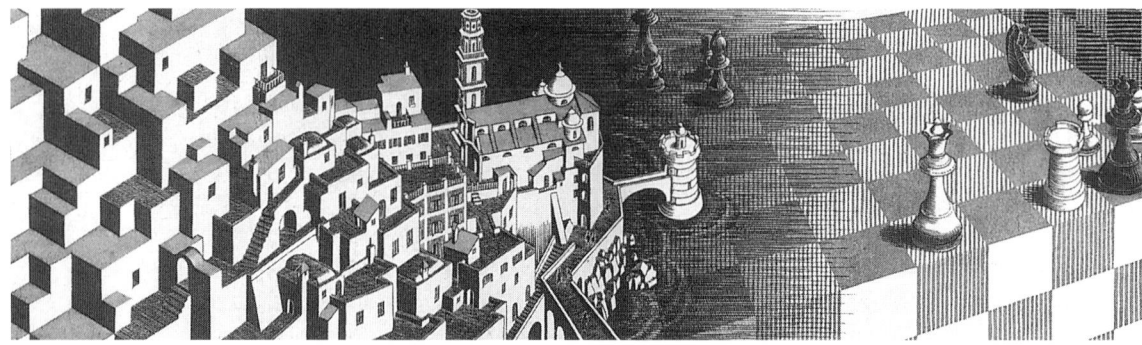

Metamorphosis II *(detail)*
Woodcut in three colors, 1939–1940

The Structure of the Plane:
Metamorphoses

The plane is mysteriously obstinate when we want to fill it up with contiguous identical figures. This can be accomplished in only seventeen different ways. Escher's interest in the regular division of planes, which he filled with periodic patterns, began early in his career. But he only incorporated these patterns in various different ways in his prints, without ever turning them into independent prints. His objective for the metamorphosis prints was to make periodic patterns undergo gradual changes. The initial shapes in this woodcut **(Metamorphosis II, 1939-1940)** are small squares. They gradually change into various animal figures such as birds, fish and reptiles. Eventually, they become an image of the town of Atrani. Here we have reproduced only one part of this three-color woodcut, which is almost thirteen feet long.

29

★

30

★

31

★

★

★

★

★

Cycle
Lithograph, 1938

The Structure of the Plane:
Cycles

A cycle is a metamorphosis whose
beginning and end are linked. In
this lithograph from 1938 titled
Cycle, Escher used a periodic
pattern, which can be seen in the
bottom part of the print. But the
cycle itself begins in the upper
right-hand corner, where a
dwarflike little man comes dashing
out of the small building. As he
runs down the stairs, he gradually
changes into a pattern of small
abstract figures in black, white and
gray that fill up the plane. On their
way up, these figures change into
rhombuses, which then form piles
of blocks and, higher still, change
into a tile floor. In the rear part of
the small building, they undergo a
metamorphosis, which is not
visible to the viewer, with the
result that the dwarflike little man
appears again. And so on.

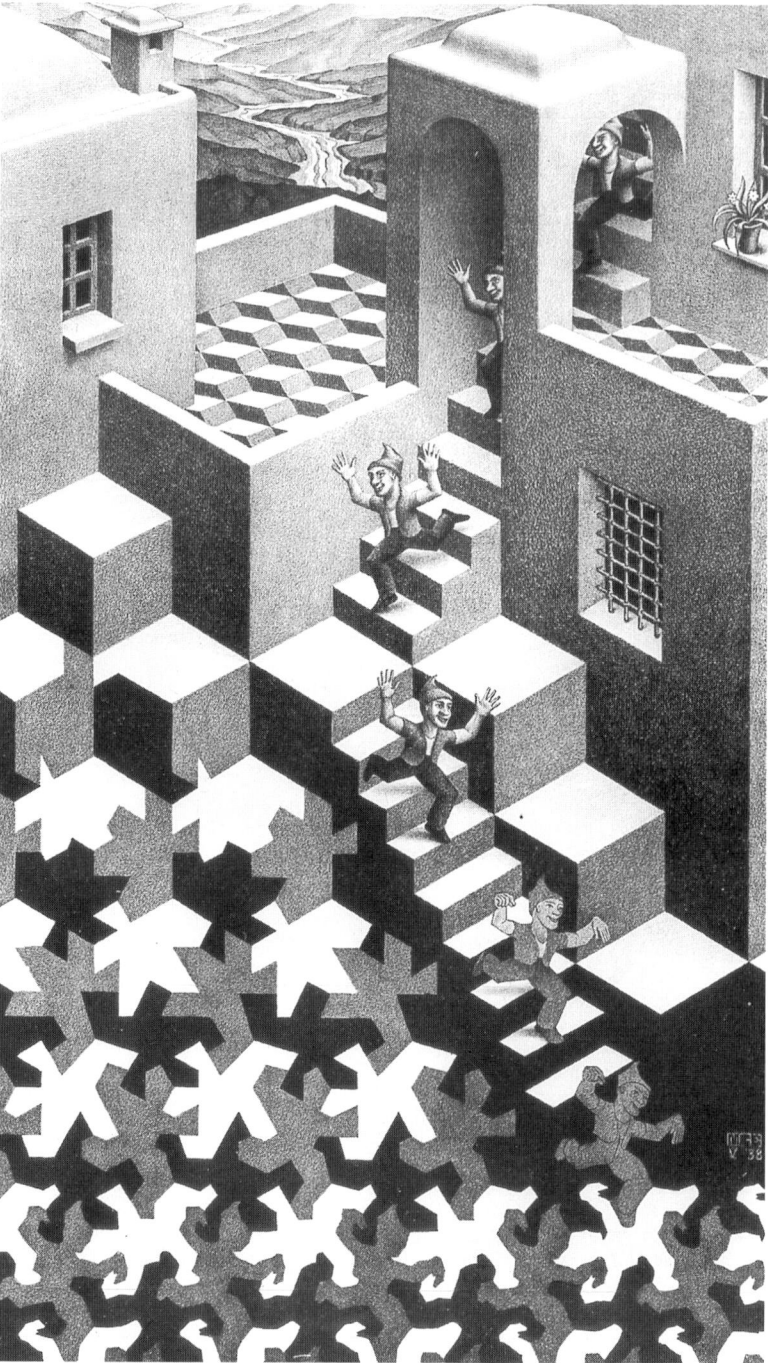

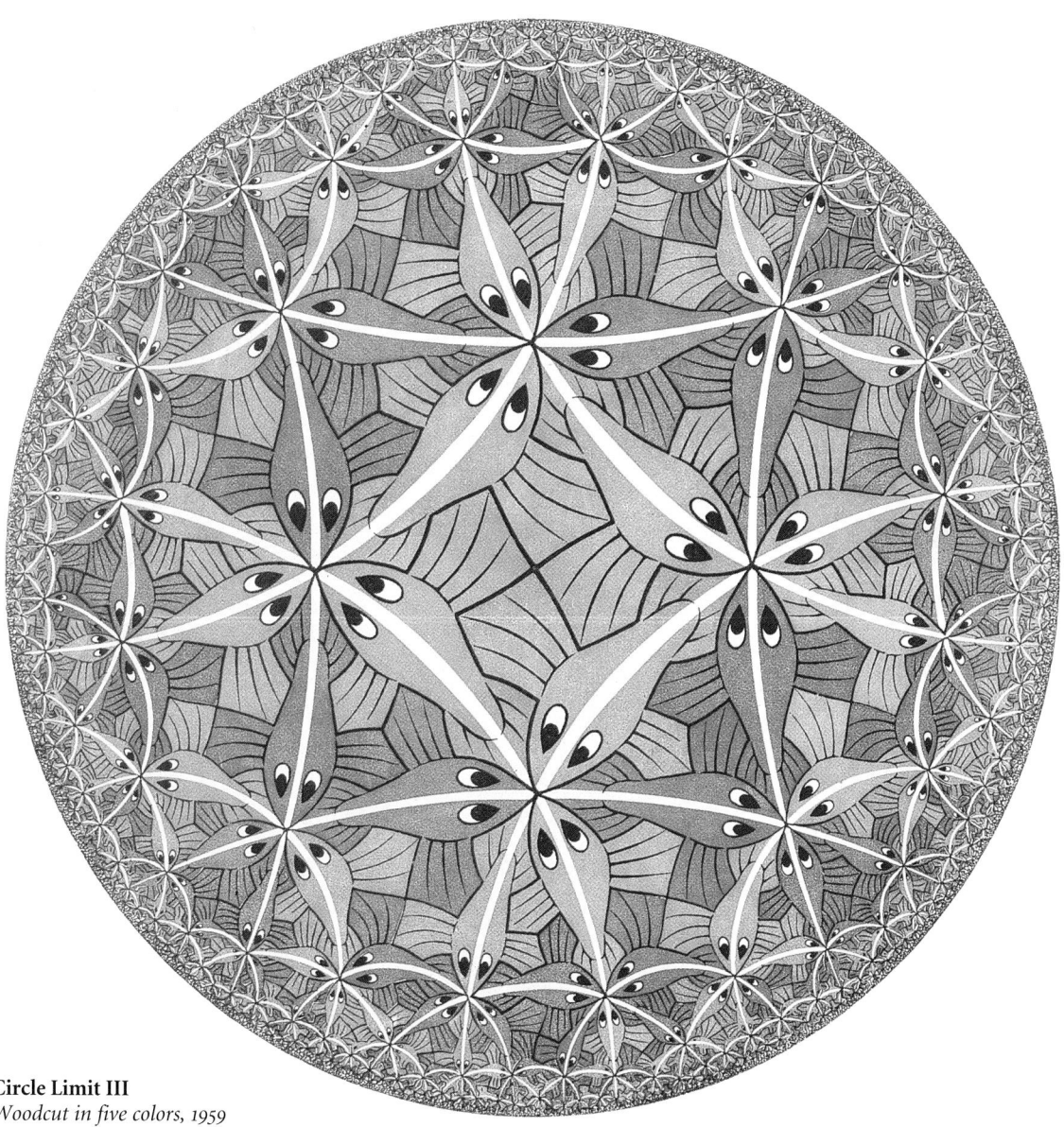

Circle Limit III
Woodcut in five colors, 1959

The Structure of the Plane:
Approaches to Infinity
All of the drawings in Escher's sketchbook that show planes filled with periodic patterns are really approaches to infinity. Each presents a piece of a plane that can continue in the same manner to stretch on into infinity. But in some later pieces, Escher wanted to represent the infinite within a finite area of a plane. To do this,

the figures had to become ever smaller so that the infinite—which, obviously, cannot ever be drawn in its entirety—could be implied on a finite surface. One of his most beautiful prints is this 1959 woodcut in five colors titled *Circle Limit III*. It shows four series of fish that become ever smaller as they swim around. Each fish starts out infinitely small at the edge and reaches its largest size

in the center. It then gets smaller and smaller again as it approaches the edge, until it becomes a mere point in an infinite series. Escher derived the layout for this print from a publication by H. Coxeter, a professor at Ottawa University in Canada, whom he had met in 1954.

Dragon
Wood engraving, 1952

Depicting Space on a Flat Surface:
The Essence of Making an Image
In this 1952 wood engraving titled
Dragon, Escher made fun of
images in general. He shows here
that every image, no matter how
skillfully it suggests a spatial
object, remains a flat image. In the
drawing of the dragon, two
horizontal cuts have been made.
The dragon pokes his head
through one of the cuts and his tail
through the other one below it.
His tail is in his mouth as he bites
into it, and we clearly experience
the dragon as a spatial creature.
But that is not possible: if it were,
the illustrator would not have been
able to make a horizontal cut into
such a creature.

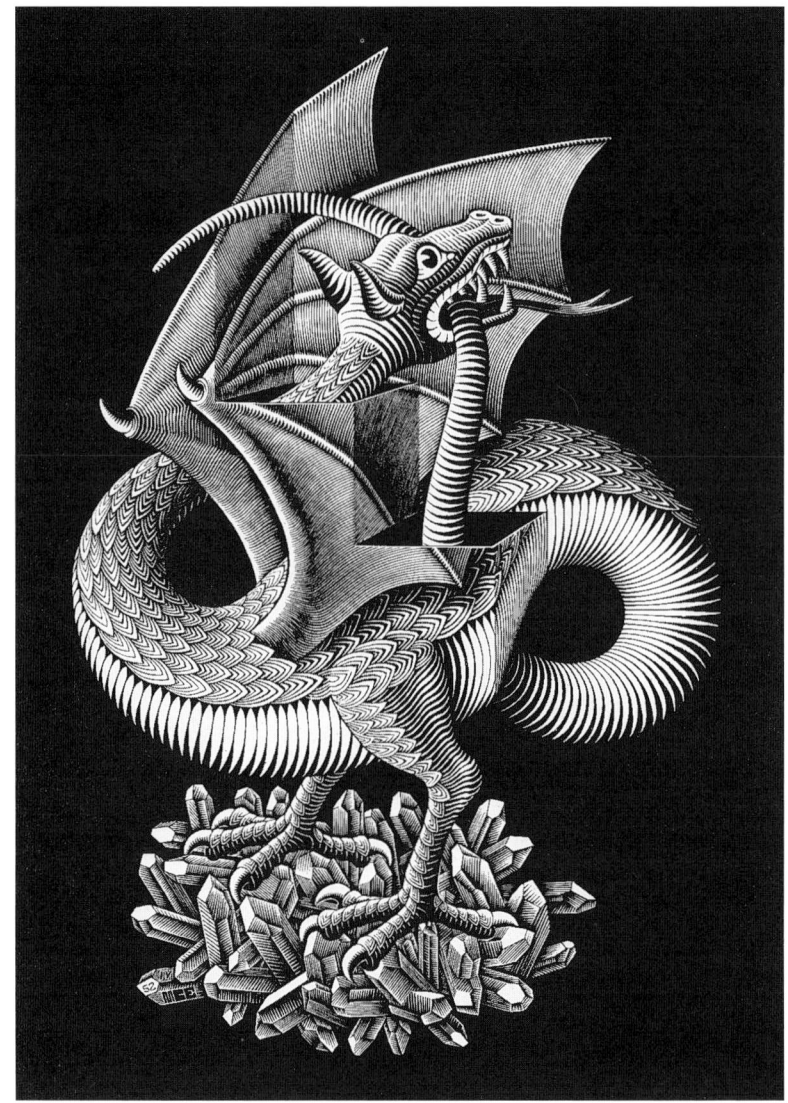

1

$\star$

2

$\star$

3

$\star$

4

$\star$

5

$\star$

6

$\star$

7

$\star$

High and Low
Lithograph, 1947

Depicting Space on a Flat Surface:
Perspective

The classic technique of perspective is an excellent tool for representing space on a flat surface. Escher discovered that using straight perspective lines is not the only nor even the best way of doing this. He experimented with curved lines, as in the lithograph **High and Low**, created in 1947. This print invites us to wander around in it. We start at the bottom, on a small square that could be located somewhere in an Italian town. To the right, there is a staircase going down. To the left is a staircase going up, and on it sits a boy who looks at a girl leaning out the window of her home. Maybe they are talking to each other; maybe this is a first, timid getting to know each other. As we move on up, we look up at a tiled ceiling. But this turns out to be the floor of the upper part of the drawing; furthermore, this floor is exactly the same as the one in the lower part of the drawing. The entire scene is then repeated again, but this time as seen from above. The towerlike building at center right must be very strange inside. Somewhere in the middle of a room, up and down must change places! The question is, does the girl see two boys on two staircases? In his preliminary sketches, Escher had at first opted for straight perspective lines and two different scenes. This would have been interesting as well, but not as ingenious as the option on which he decided for the final lithograph.

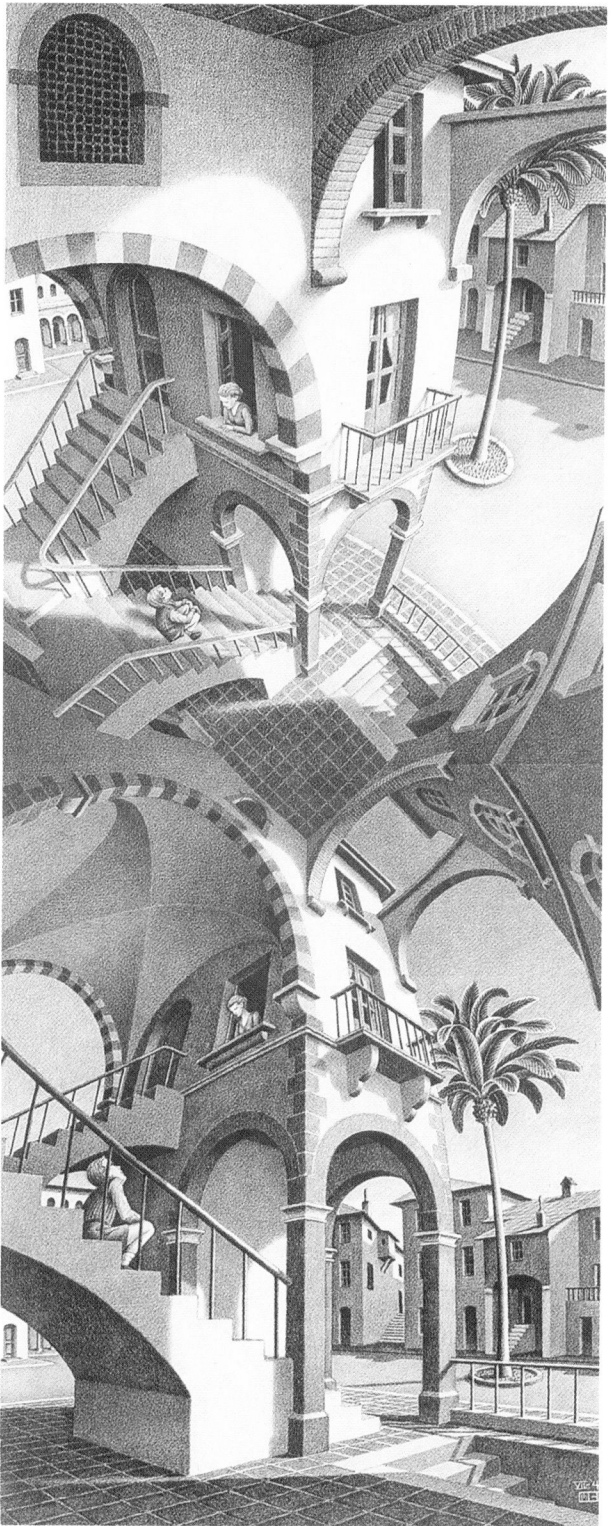

8   ⋆

9   ⋆

10   ⋆

11   ⋆

12   ⋆

13   ⋆

14   ⋆

Belvédère
Lithograph, 1958

Depicting Space on a Flat Surface:
Impossible Figures

Every spatial object can in some way be depicted on a plane. The opposite, however, is not true: not every image portraying some part of space can actually be built in space. Such images are known as "impossible figures." Escher invented one himself and called it the "impossible cube." The boy sitting on the bench to the left in **Belvédère** has just such an impossible cube in his hands. It is a cube that cannot exist, and this fact is illustrated by the print as a whole. The middle floor of the structure is one of these impossible cubes. Going from top to bottom, its pillars start at the back of the building but end at the front. The upper floor seems to be perpendicular to the middle floor, but the stepladder is simultaneously inside and outside the building. Yet at first sight there is nothing wrong with this building, which could be part of a princely palace built somewhere in the mountains of Italy.

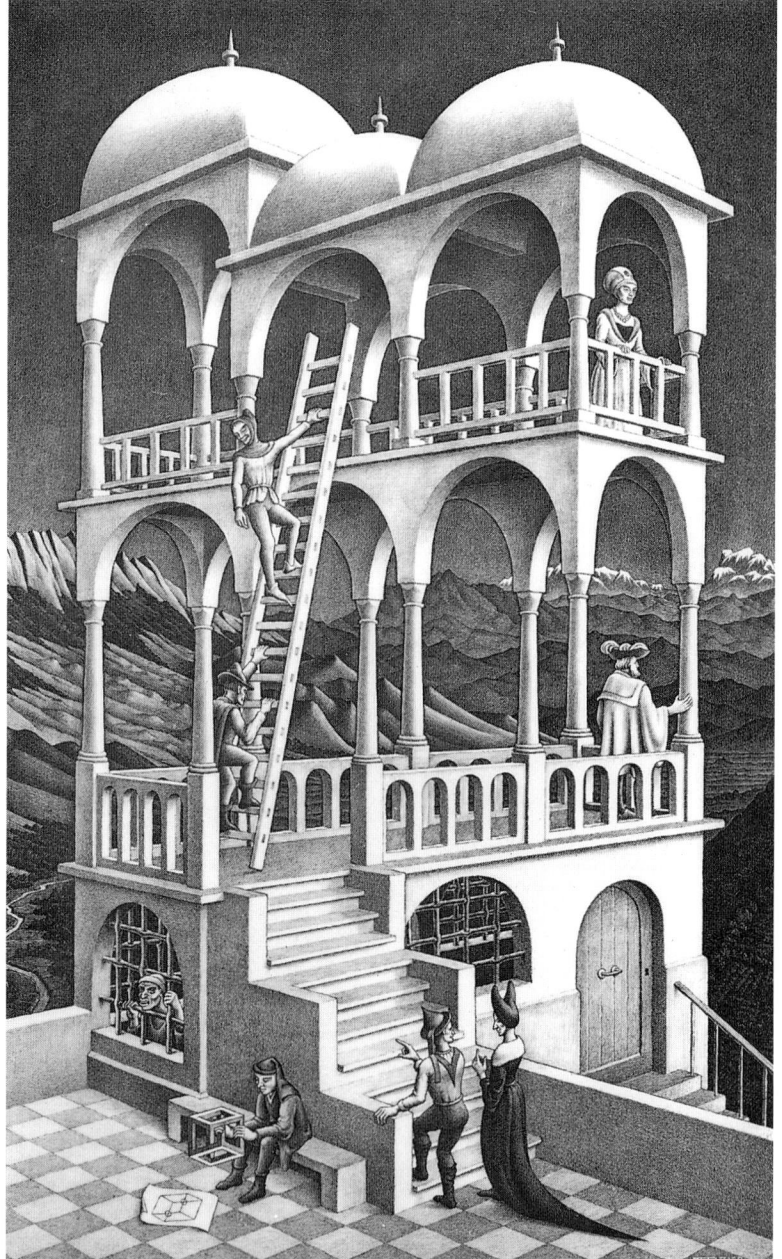

15

★

16

★

17

★

18

★

19

★

20

★

21

★

22   ⋆

23   ⋆

24   ⋆

25   ⋆

26   ⋆

27   ⋆

28   29   ⋆

Portrait of G. A. Escher
Lithograph (counterproof), 1935

Maurits Cornelis Escher was born in the city of Leeuwarden in 1898. He was the son of G. A. Escher, a civil engineer, by his second wife. Escher's stepbrother, called "Bear" by family and friends, became a well-known professor in mineralogy, crystallography, geology and paleontology at the University of Leiden and wrote several important textbooks. Father Escher worked in Osaka, Japan, for five years, a period he considered the most fascinating of his life. The portrait on this page, made by Escher in 1935, was really meant only for members of the family. It is a lithograph counterproof, a technique whereby a wet copy is definitively printed on another sheet after the lithograph is printed.

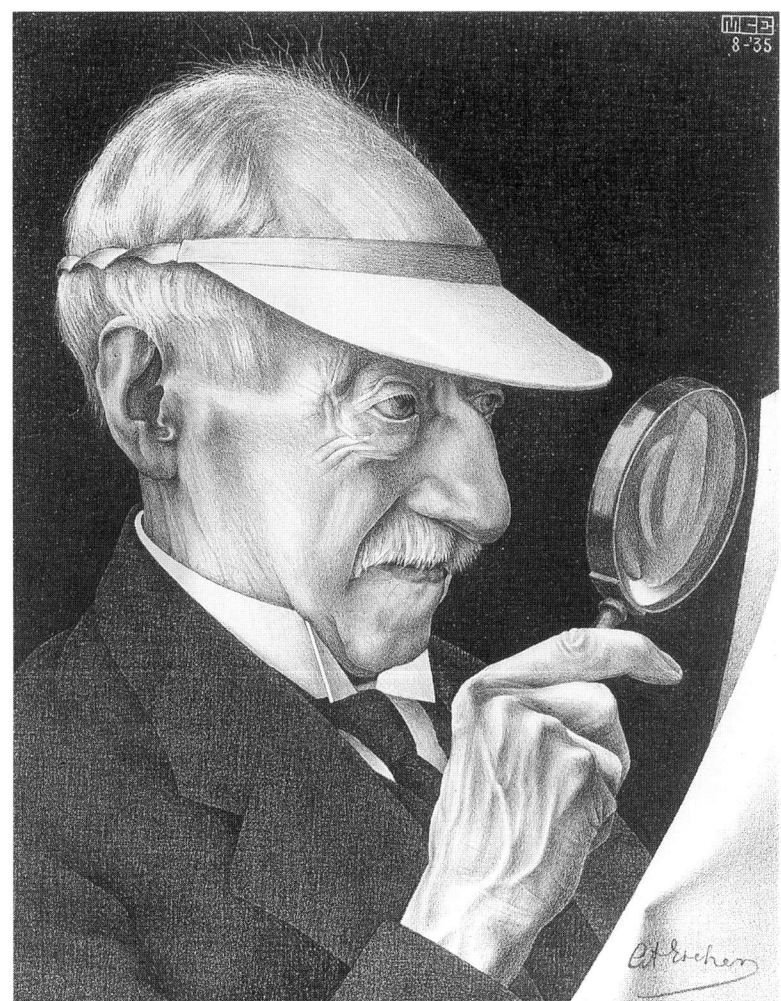

1898	Escher is born in Leeuwarden.
1912-1918	Receives his high school education at the HBS in Arnhem.
1919-1922	Studies at the School for Architectural and Decorative Arts in Haarlem.
1922	Travels for more than two months through the north of Italy and then takes a trip to Spain. He subsequently lives in Siena for a while.

Portrait of Escher as a Youth

When Escher was five years old,
his family moved to Arnhem. Two
years later, for health reasons, he
spent a year in the coastal resort of
Zandvoort aan Zee. His high
school education in Arnhem
proceeded with difficulty. He had
problems with mathematical
subjects in particular, although
these were not the ones that
caused him to fail the final exam.
The drawing lessons were a relief
for him, and his most pleasant
memories were those of his
drawing teacher, F. W. van der
Haagen. Escher's earliest prints
date from his high school years.
The photograph on this page was
taken in 1913, during a family
vacation spent in Brittany, France.

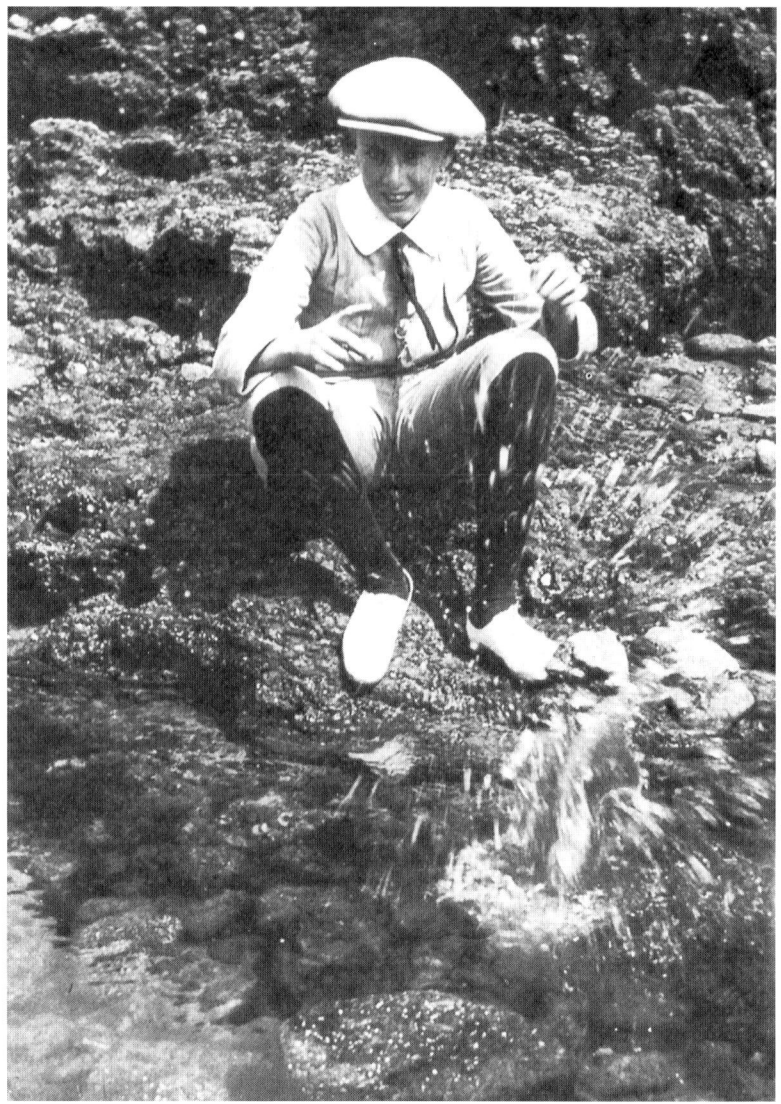

1
     ★

2
     ★

3
     ★

4
     ★

5
     ★

6
     ★

7
     ★

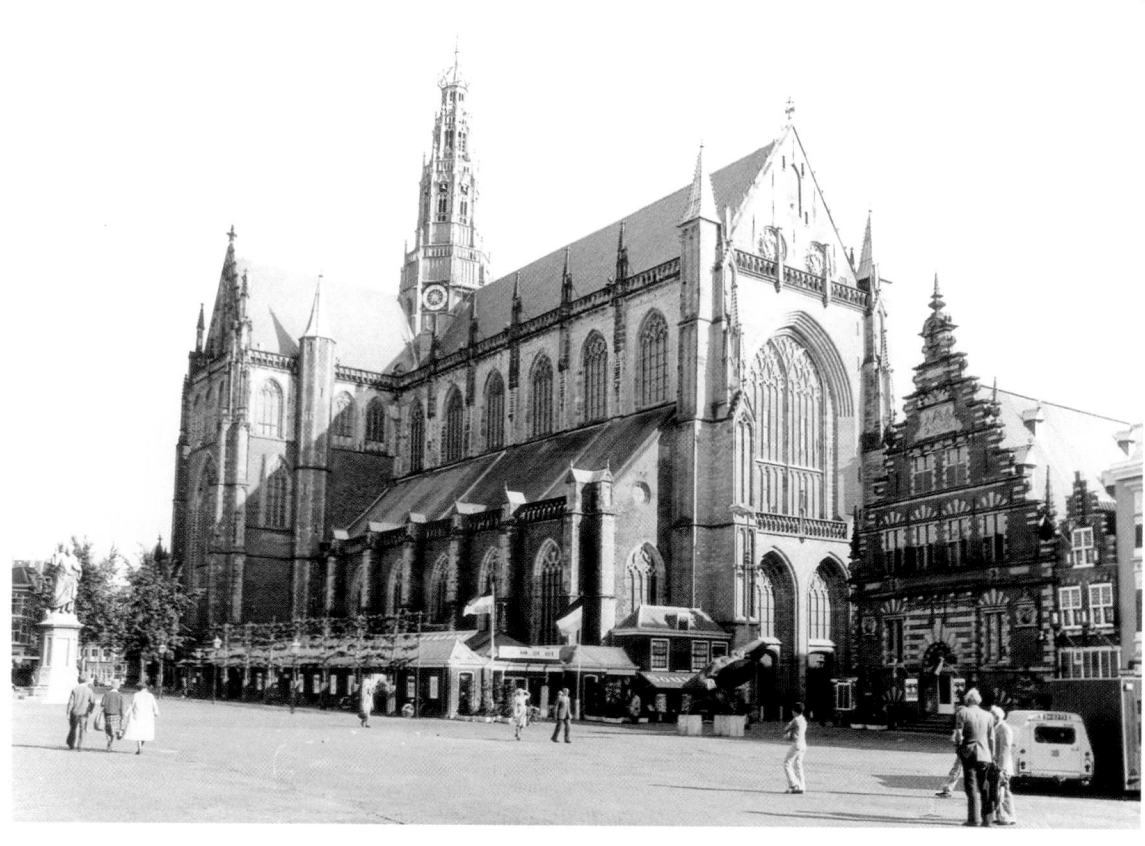

The Old Saint Bavo Cathedral in Haarlem

Escher's parents had hoped that Mauk, as he was called by friends and family, would pursue university studies in science. After he failed his high school exam, however, it became much more difficult to turn this hope into a reality. It was decided that he would take private lessons from a tutor. Permission was also obtained from the president of the College of Engineering in Delft for him to start attending classes there at the same time. But he got so far behind due to illness that he had to give up this idea. The alternative of studying architecture at the School for Architectural and Decorative Arts in Haarlem was then considered, and he moved to Haarlem in September 1919. At this school, drawing was taught by Jessurun de Mesquita, to whom Escher showed his drawings and linocuts. In consultation with the director of the school, Mr. Verkruysen, Escher was advised by de Mesquita to abandon the idea of studying architecture and to concentrate on drawing and the graphic arts. His parents agreed.

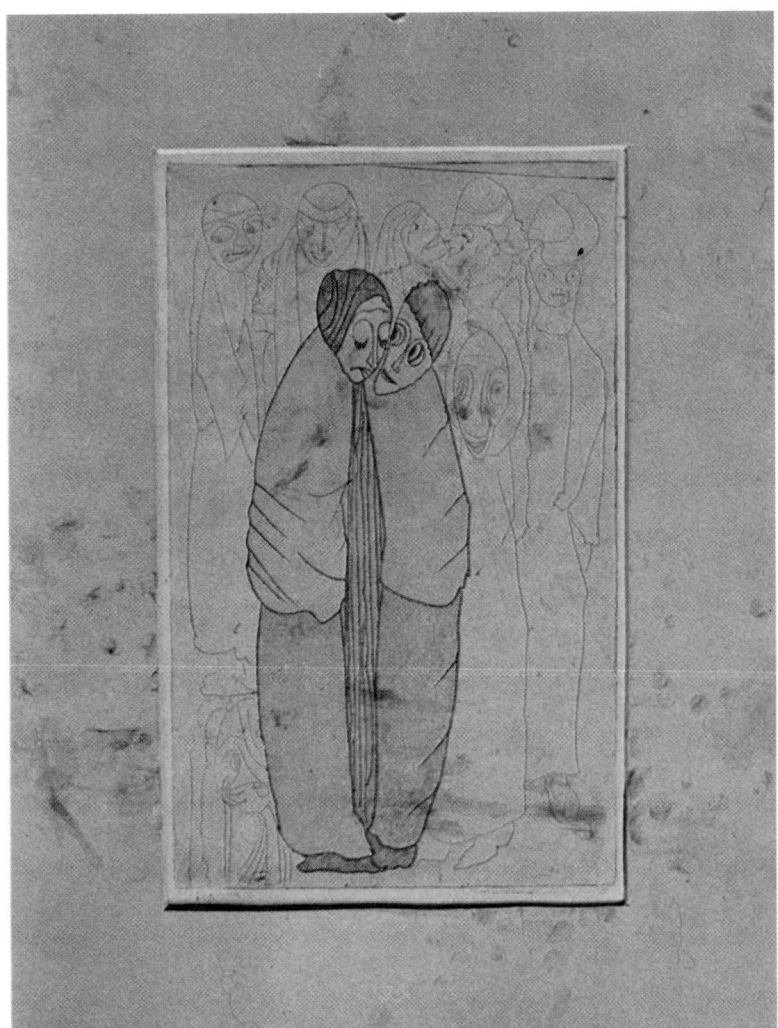

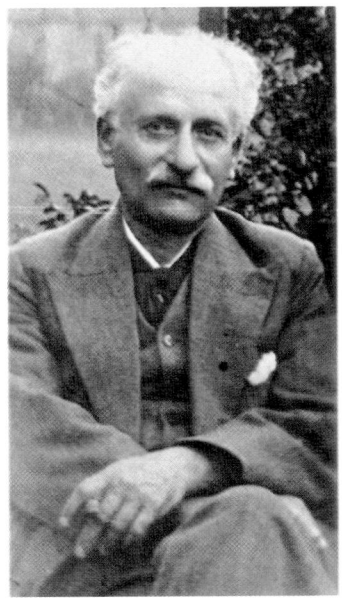

**Portrait of Jessurun de Mesquita;
print by de Mesquita**

Escher wrote to one of his friends about his teachers: "Mr. Jessurun is a little Jewish guy, extremely likeable . . . , very sharp and alert. As you know, he is a real expert in the graphic arts, especially in woodcuts. The school has several other nice teachers, all very bright. One of them is the director, Mr. Verkruysen, who is a philosopher by profession and who teaches composition."

Jessurun de Mesquita was an accomplished artist with an experimental approach to art. Escher did not adopt this approach from his teacher, but he did learn excellent woodcut techniques from him. He and de Mesquita also became lifelong friends.

When the de Mesquita family was forced from their home and taken away by the Germans in 1944, Escher took the majority of his teacher's prints to the Stedelijk Museum in Amsterdam for safekeeping. He kept only one print, which had been soiled by the boot of a German soldier (see above).

Escher's teachers never did consider him a promising artist. When he left the school, his records contained the following remarks: "He is too conservative and has too much of a literary and philosophical bent; he is not a young man who gives in to his moods and impulses; he is not enough of an artist."

Interior of Saint Bavo Cathedral
Pen-and-ink drawing, 1920

The curriculum at the school in
Haarlem took barely two years to
complete, but Escher's hard work
and passion for drawing allowed
him to make the most of the brief
period of study. He did this pen-
and-ink drawing of the interior of
Saint Bavo's in Haarlem in 1920.
He was particularly fascinated by
the reflection of the entire church
in the copper globe of a
chandelier. He tried to portray this
as accurately as possible, even to
the point of drawing himself
standing in the church with his
drawing pad. Viewed with his later
work in mind, this drawing is an
important indication of his
developing interest. Reflecting
spheres would continue to intrigue
him with their apparent ability to
allow two different objects to be in
the same place at the same time—
in this case, both the shiny sphere
and the entire cathedral.

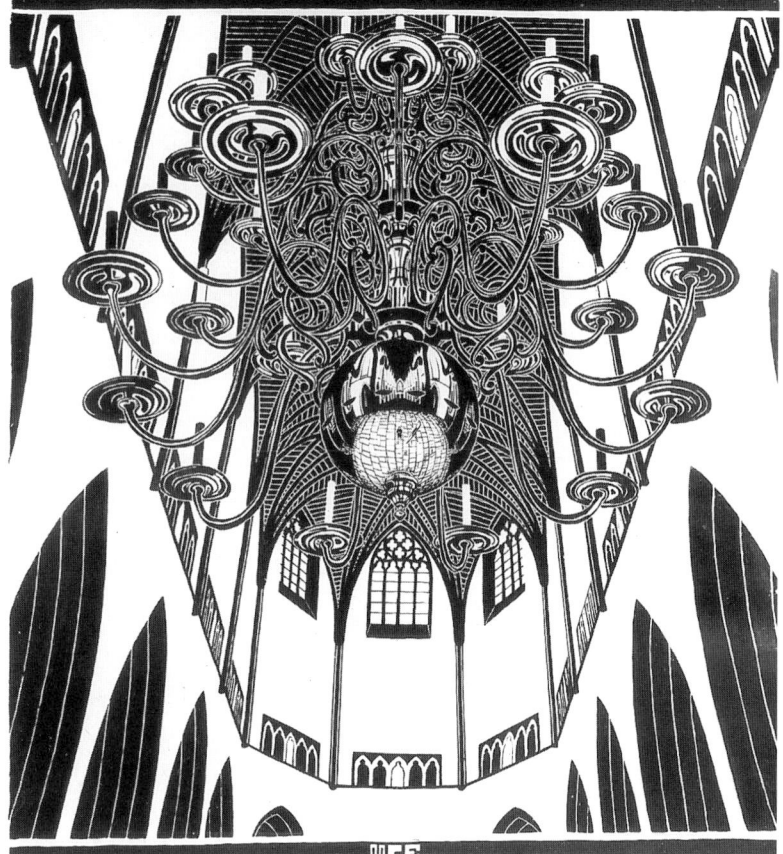

| 8 | ⋆ |

| 9 | ⋆ |

| 10 | ⋆ |

| 11 | ⋆ |

| 12 | ⋆ |

| 13 | ⋆ |

| 14 | ⋆ |

March

15　　　　　　　　　　　　　　　★

16　　　　　　　　　　　　　　　★

17　　　　　　　　　　　　　　　★

18　　　　　　　　　　　　　　　★

19　　　　　　　　　　　　　　　★

20　　　　　　　　　　　　　　　★

21　　　　　　　　　　　　　　　★

Four Woodcuts from the Book
Flor de Pascua (*1921*)

In 1921, during his brief sojourn as
a student, Escher illustrated a small
book with twenty-six woodcuts.
The book, titled *Flor de Pascua
(Easter Flower)*, was written by Aad
van Stolk, a friend of Escher's. It
contained texts that were partly
philosophical and partly a
mockery. This series of small
prints is particularly interesting in
light of the work Escher produced
later. In **The Scapegoat** we detect
his feeling for symmetry and
reflection. The rooster and the
mother nursing her child are
simply from the school of de
Mesquita. The reflecting sphere,
however, is a precursor of a
number of such spheres that
Escher would create after 1935.

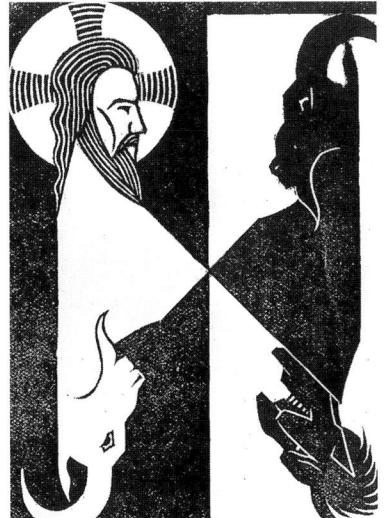

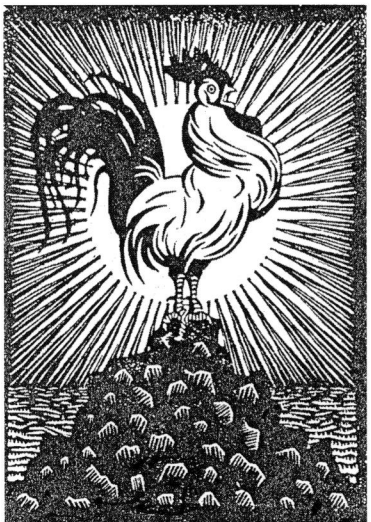

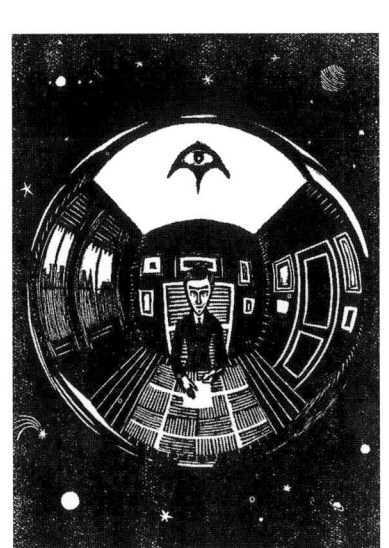

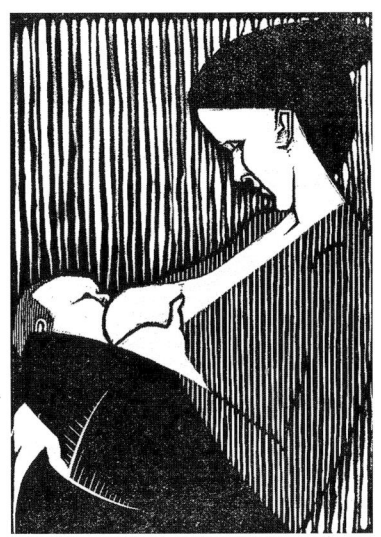

Photograph of an Alley Below Street Level in the Town of Atrani

After his years in Haarlem, Escher began traveling. He traveled mainly in the Mediterranean region, where he dedicated himself to studying art. He admired the works of the Italian Renaissance artists and, in particular, the Italian landscape, which inspired him to produce a large number of sketches and prints. Of the thirteen years during which he lived in Italy, he spent about three and a half traveling! He was most fascinated by complicated structures, such as a covered alley (which I managed to locate after a seemingly endless search) in the town of Atrani, south of Naples.

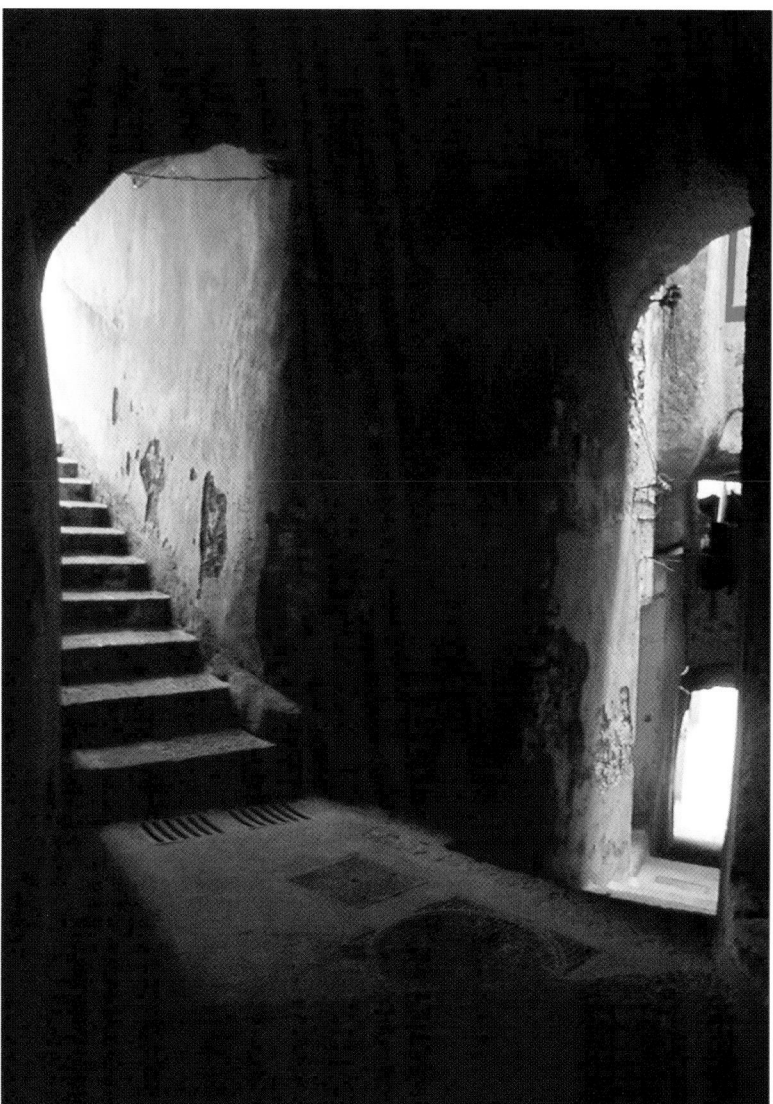

1923	Escher holds his first solo exhibition in Siena. Meets his future wife, Jetta Umiker, in Ravello.
1924	Marries Jetta and, from 1925 on, lives in Rome.
1926	First son, George, is born.
1928	Takes a hiking trip through the Abruzzi Mountains; son Arthur is born.
1935	Settles in Switzerland and, two years later, in Belgium (in the town of Ukkel).
1938	Youngest son, Jan, is born.

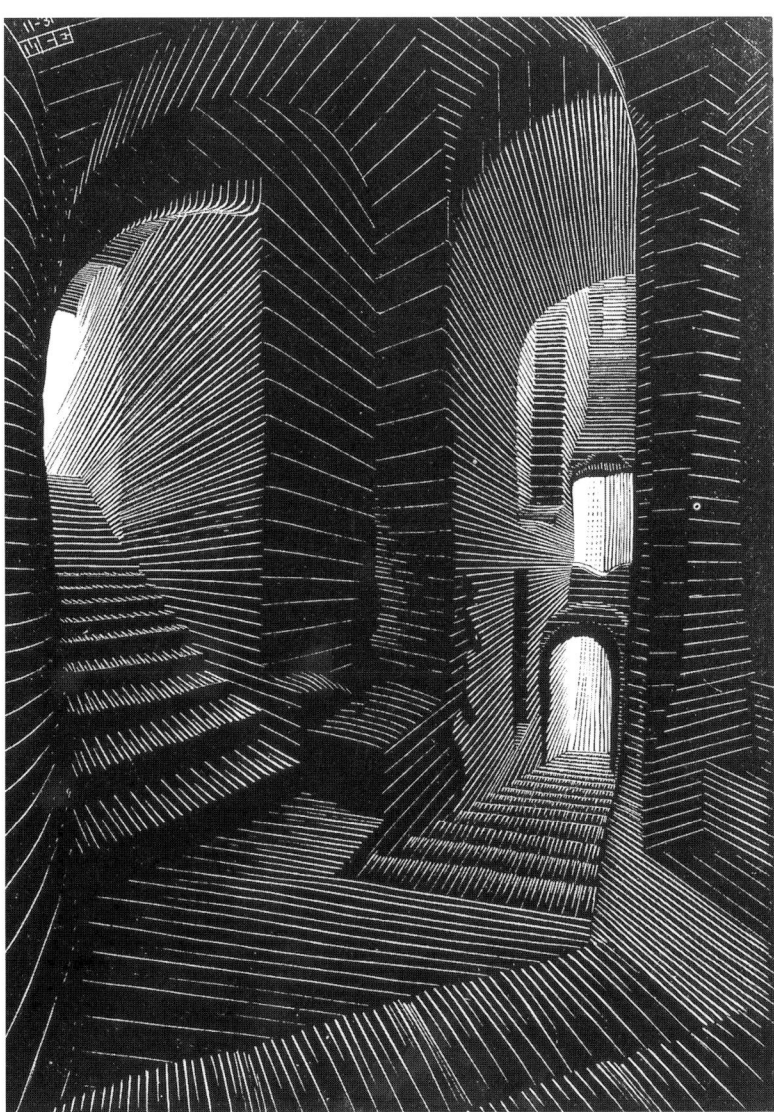

Covered Alley in Atrani
Wood engraving, 1931

During his stay in Italy, Escher generally traveled from early spring through summer, during which time he mainly did landscape sketches. He then turned the most suitable ones into woodcuts or lithographs during the fall and winter.

In September 1931, he made this wood engraving of one of the many alleys in Atrani that are practically underground. He had been doing a lot of drawing there during the spring, while he lived nearby. Altogether, his stay in the area of Atrani produced fifteen prints!

22   ✲

23   ✲

24   ✲

25   ✲

26   ✲

27   ✲

28   ✲

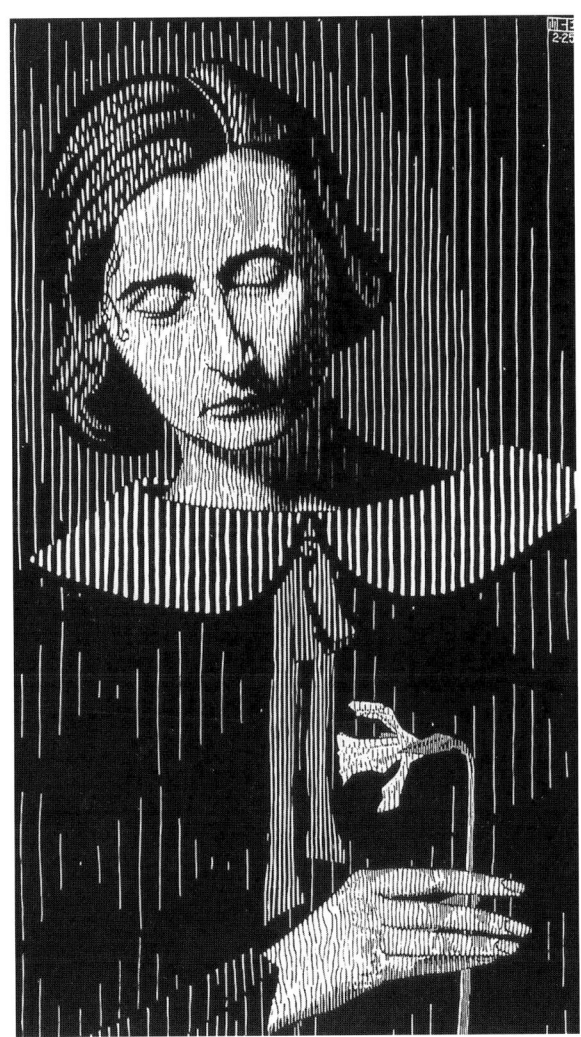

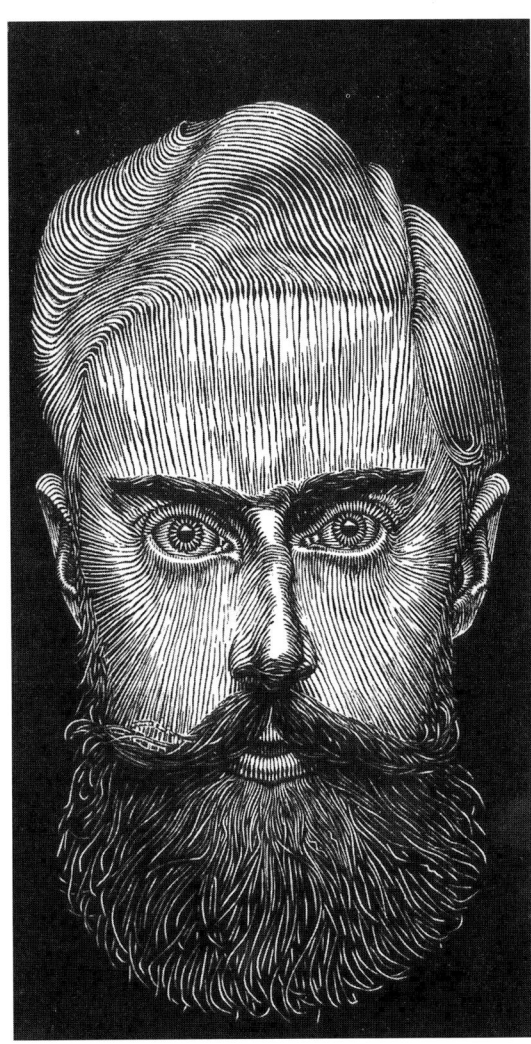

Portrait of Jetta
Woodcut, 1925
Self-Portrait
Woodcut, 1923

In 1923, Escher had taken lodgings in Ravello, a mountain village on the coast of Amalfi. A couple of weeks after his arrival, the Swiss industrialist Umiker came to stay in the same pension, along with his wife and his daughter, Jetta. Escher fell in love with Jetta. He wrote to his friend Jan: "Next to me, at the little table on which I have my papers, a 25-year-old girl is sitting. At the moment, she is busy eating a cookie, and seeing this, I am suddenly extremely moved." Later he wrote: "The girl about whom I wrote you a few days ago has left for Switzerland with her parents. She exerted an influence on me that was similar to that of an electromagnet on an insignificant piece of pig iron."

Just before the Umikers left, Escher declared his love to Jetta, and a year later they were married. In 1925, Escher made a splendid woodcut of Jetta, reproduced here next to a self-portrait he had done two years earlier.

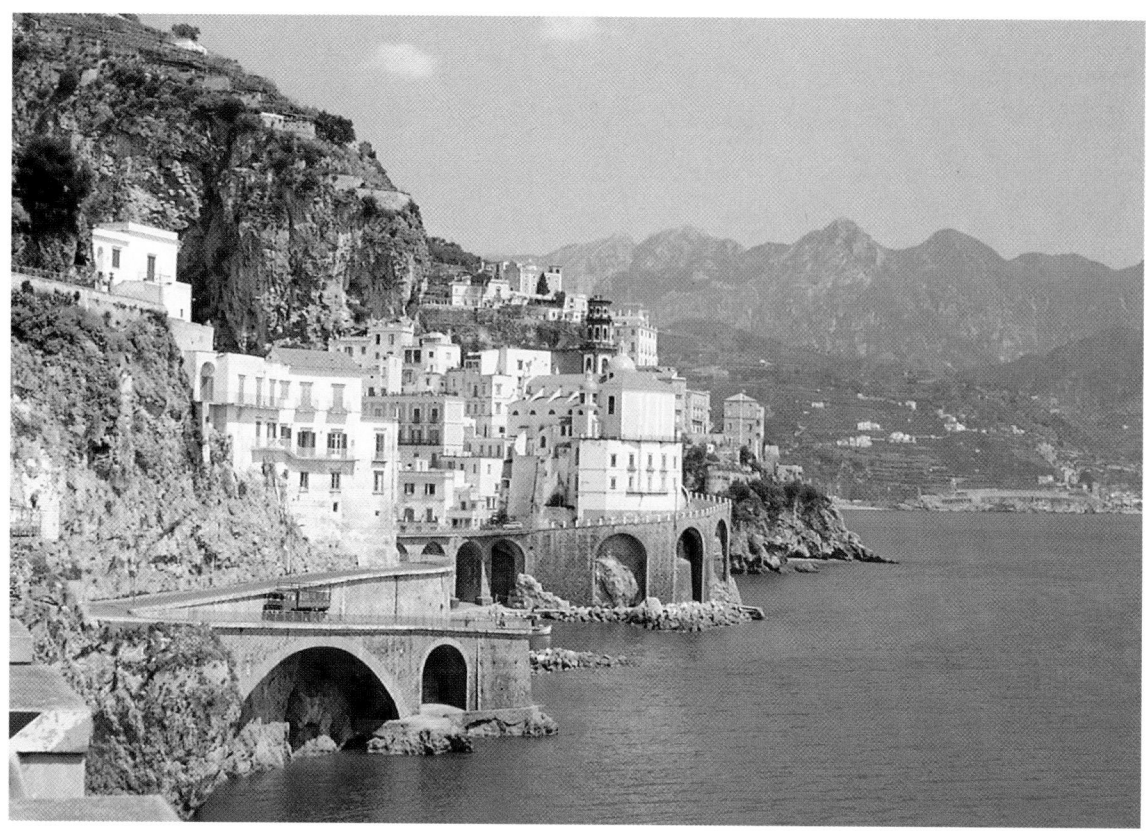

Photograph of the Coast of Amalfi

South of Naples, between Sorrento and Salerno, there is a coastal area more than thirty miles long where the mountains descend rather steeply to the sea. One of the fishing villages nestled at the foot of these mountains is Amalfi. But Amalfi has the air of a small city—a Renaissance city, that is. It boasts a cathedral and a bishop's palace, and on religious holidays the people still observe their elaborate folkloric customs. Escher witnessed such celebrations several times. Amalfi was also an important harbor, and the town was renowned for its paper mills, one of which is still operating.

It was this part of Italy that Escher loved most of all. Was it because he first met his wife in Ravello, situated in the mountains about six miles from Amalfi? One reason was certainly the unequaled beauty of this coastal area. In the sketches he made at the coast of Amalfi, we can already see elements he later incorporated in his mathematical prints.

29   ★

30   ★

31   ★

★

★

★

★

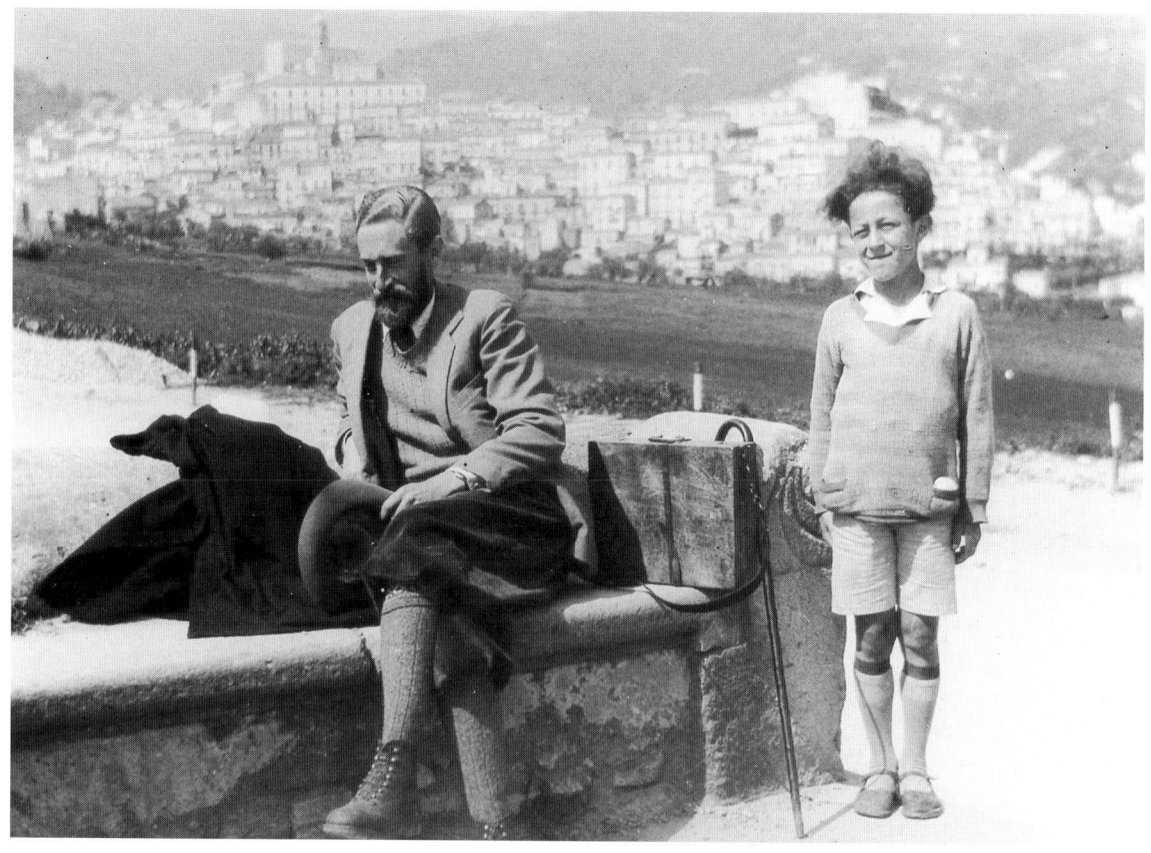

Escher During One of His Many Travels

The period during which the Eschers lived in Rome was a very happy one for the young couple. Their sons George and Arthur were born there, and Escher became extremely productive and experienced his first successes as his work began to be appreciated. The couple would have liked to live in Frascati, but they could not find a suitable house there. In Rome, they bought the second floor of a house that was being built on the slopes of the Monte Verde. But the house, at 100 Via Allessandro Poerio, was too damp and too small. Fortunately, they managed to find a suitable place nearby, at number 94. Escher had his studio, which we see in the print *Hand with Reflecting Sphere* (see page 12), on the fourth floor.

1

★

2

★

3

★

4

★

5

★

6

★

7

★

Woodcut from the Book
Scholastica (1932)

Escher proved to be an excellent illustrator. In 1931, the director of the Dutch Historical Institute in Rome, art historian G. J. Hoogewerff, suggested that Escher create a series of prints for a collection of short Latin proverbs, each of which would be described by a four-line rhyming verse in Dutch. Titled *Emblemata*, the book was published a year later under Hoogewerff's pseudonym, A. E. Drijfhout. In that same year, Escher began working on illustrations for a story by Jan Walch about the witch of Oudewater, titled *The Terrible Adventures of Scholastica*.

Escher's illustrations were technically perfect, as evidenced by a comparison of the woodcut on this page with those on page 35, representing his first attempts, produced for the book *Flor de Pasqua*. They excelled in their imaginative content and in the unexpected angles of sight he chose. In 1939, Escher was commissioned by the Dutch government to illustrate a small book about the city of Delft with ten woodcuts. Unfortunately, the book was not published, but the prints are true masterworks.

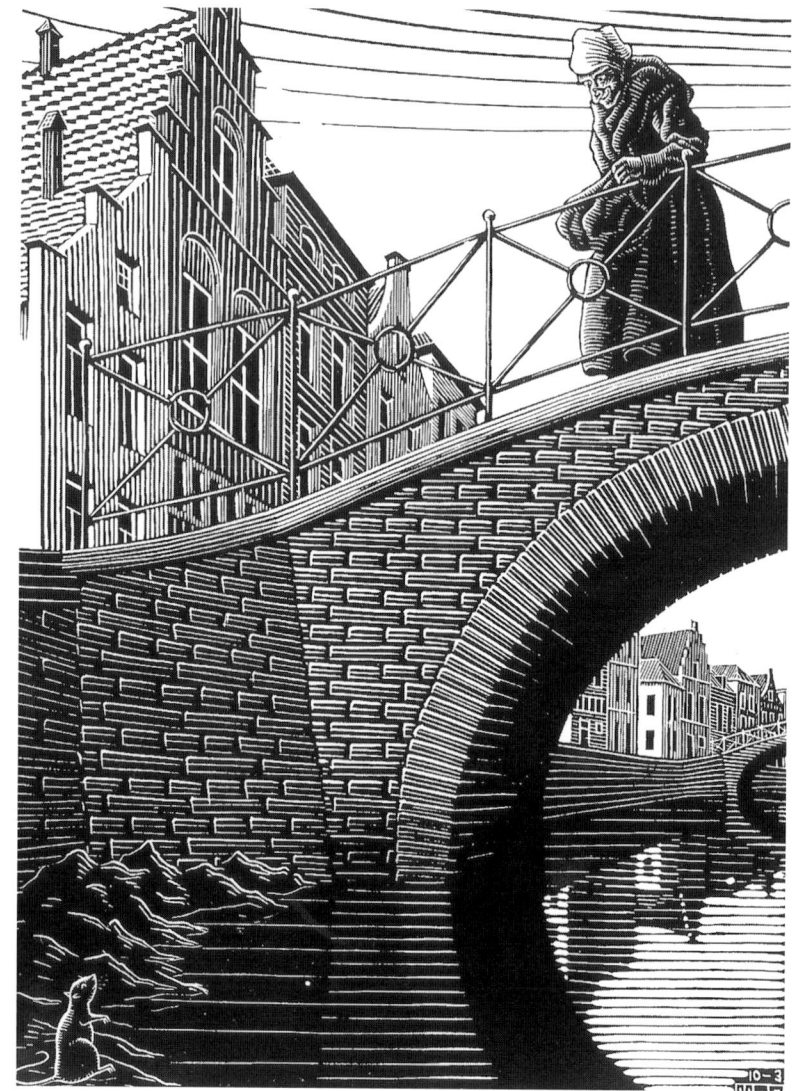

8   ⋆

9   ⋆

10   ⋆

11   ⋆

12   ⋆

13   ⋆

14   ⋆

April

Nocturnal Rome: the "Dioscuro" Pollux (Piazza del Campidoglio)
Woodcut, 1934

In 1934, Escher did a series of twelve prints with the theme **Nocturnal Rome**. His intention was not only to capture well-known views of the city but also, and more important, to attain the effect of chiaroscuro with twelve different types of shadings. He did each sketch at night and then made the woodcut on the following day. In the image reproduced on this page, we see one of the Dioscuri (Pollux, one of the twin sons of the Greek god Zeus by Leda) on the Piazza del Campidoglio. Here Escher's shading consists only of horizontal lines.

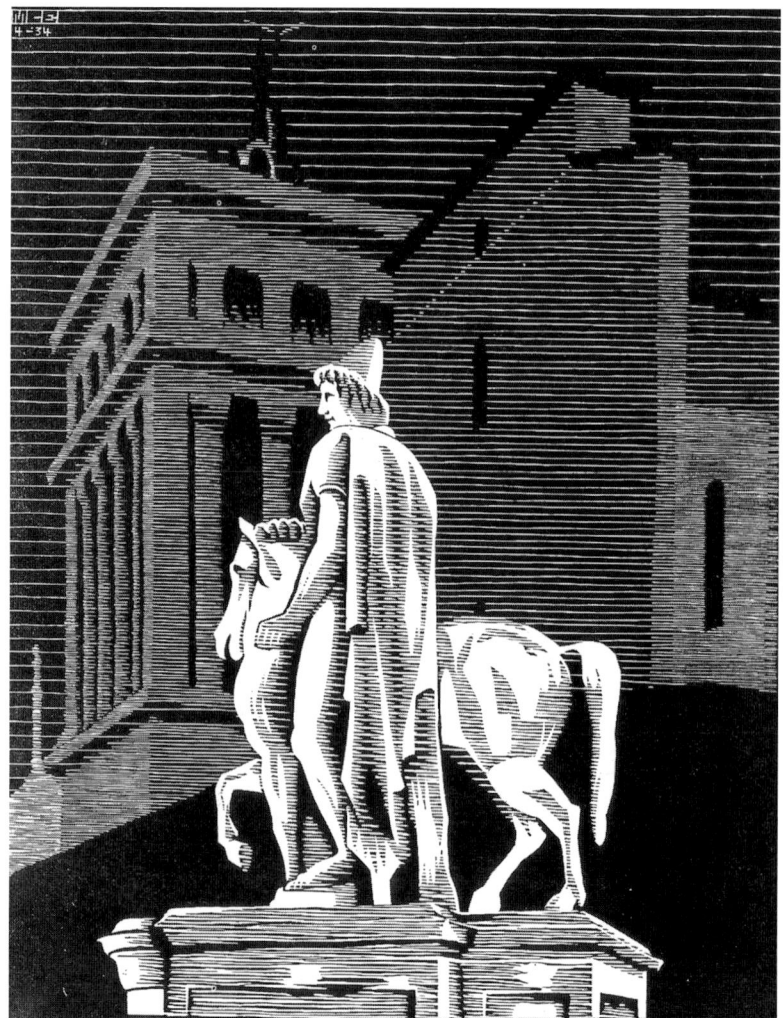

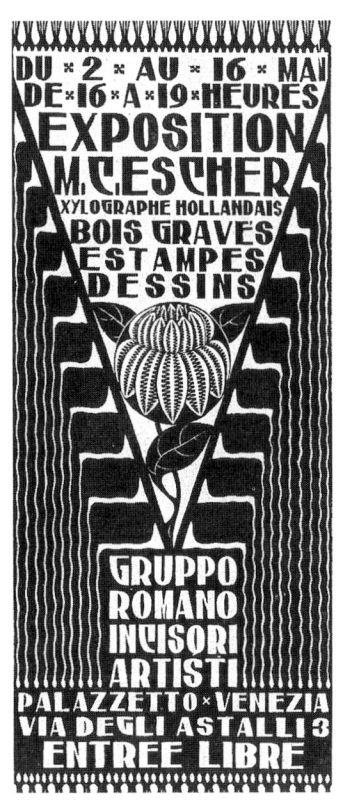

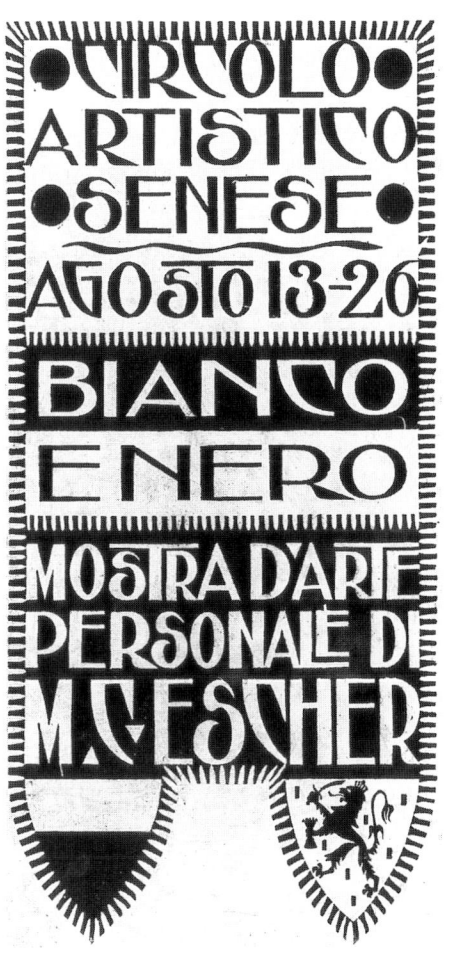

Woodcuts for Exhibitions in
Siena *(1923)* **and Rome** *(1926)*

With all the appreciation that, quite justifiably, exists for Escher's later work, we must not forget that he was a well-known and respected graphic artist long before he produced his mathematically oriented prints. In fact, he held solo exhibitions regularly. The first of these took place in Siena in 1923. Subsequently, there was a new one almost every year: The Hague in 1924, Rome in 1926, Amsterdam in 1927, Leiden in 1928, and so on. Dutch galleries with print collections purchased his work, but sales to private buyers were not insignificant. Sometimes the reviews were somewhat negative:

"His woodcuts display a dogmatic certainty as well as a cool, deliberate matter-of-factness that excludes all spontaneity" (*Rotterdamse Courant*, 1927). Appreciation of his work of this period was best summarized in an article in the *Algemeen Handelsblad* (1934): "Escher is an artist who, after very rapid development, has now reached a high point in graphic techniques, as well as in the synthetic representation of nature, from which it will be difficult to progress any further; he is a completely mature and very individual talent."

This was written before Escher began to dicover his own new world!

15   ★

16   ★

17   ★

18   ★

19   ★

20   ★

21   ★

22

*

23

*

24

*

25

*

26

*

27

*

28

*

Issued and Unissued Stamps

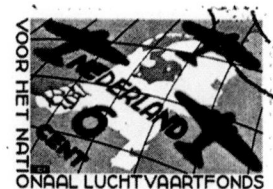

Just before his departure from Rome, Escher designed a stamp for the Dutch Postal Services (PTT) that was to benefit the National Aviation Fund. At the last check, done at Enschedé printers in

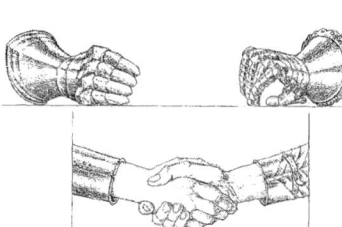

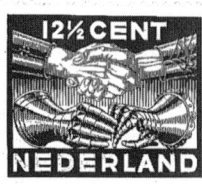

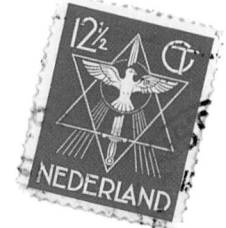

Haarlem, he chose brown as the color (issue of 336,000).

Escher had already created a design for the PTT in 1932, when he participated in a contest for the design of a peace stamp. Some sketches, as well as the ultimate result, have been preserved. Escher was one of fifteen finalists chosen from among the 817 contestants, but the design selected was the peace dove, a design by P. Hofman. In 1939, Escher made two designs for a Venezuelan airmail stamp. The second one, an image of the Caribbean region shadowed by a plane flying overhead, is particularly beautiful, but the design was never executed. In 1949, Escher designed three series of two stamps each, one brown and one blue, to commemorate the seventy-fifth anniversary of the World Postal Union. These are typical Escher designs. The Dutch issue of the ten-cent stamp consisted of almost twenty-two million, and that of the blue twenty-cent stamp numbered almost two million.

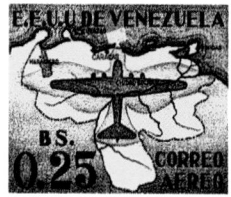

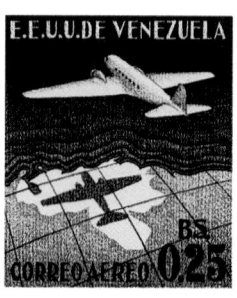

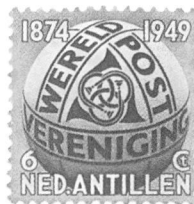

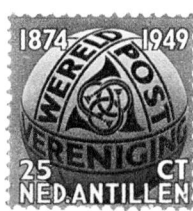

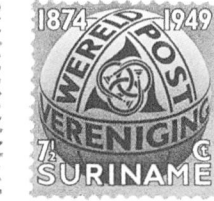

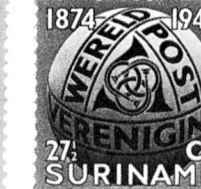

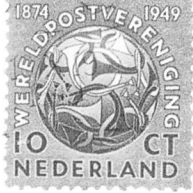

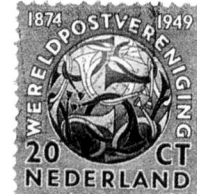

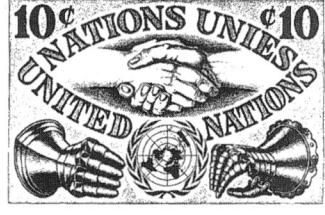

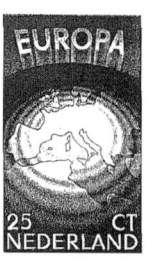

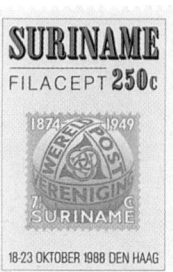

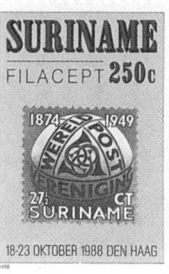

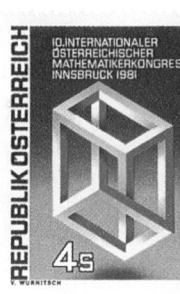

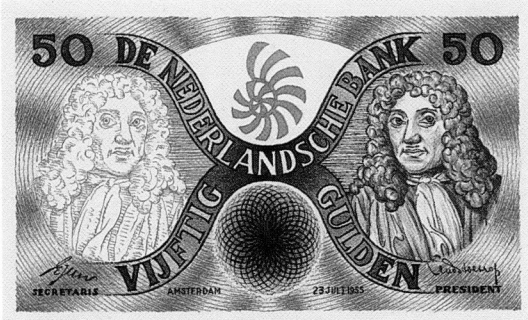

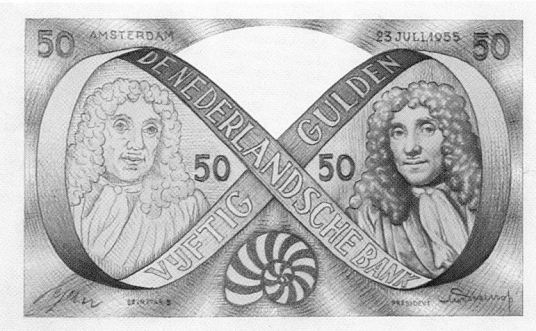

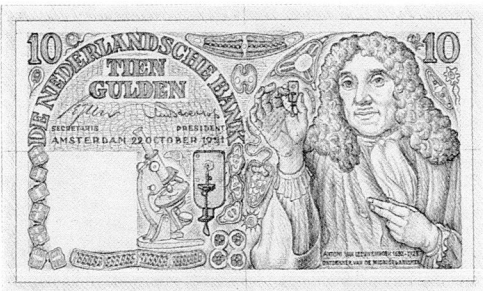

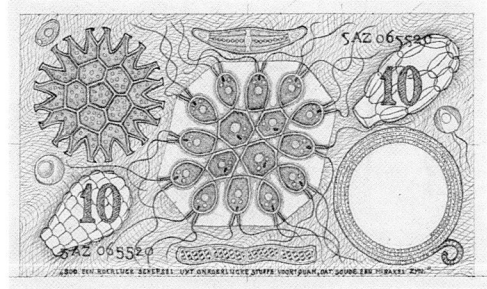

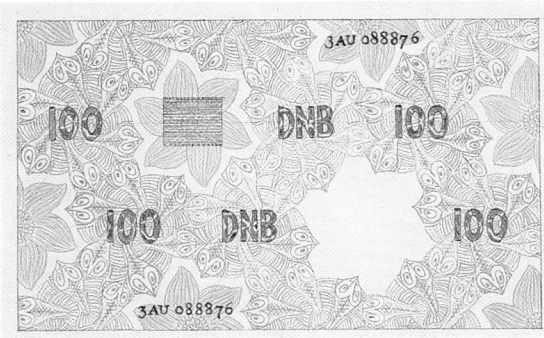

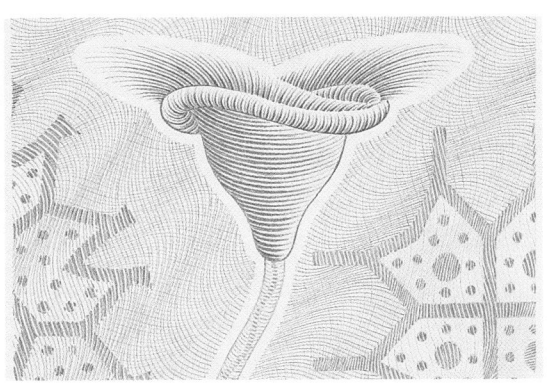

Designs for Bank Notes

In 1951, a contest was announced for a United Nations stamp. The management of Enschedé, Dutch printers of stamps and bank notes, encouraged Escher to send in a design. He did, renewing his 1932 theme of the contrast between armor-clad hands and a friendly handshake (see page 50). His design, however, was not used. Escher's last stamp design, also not executed, was the Europe stamp of 1956. The design was similar to previous ones, on which part of

the earth can be seen from space. There are two more stamps, which could be called posthumous. On the occasion of the International Mathematicians Congress in Innsbruck in 1981, a stamp was issued on which an "impossible cube" was depicted (the one and only "impossible" figure Escher himself ever invented). In 1988, two stamps of Fl 2.50 each were issued in Surinam on the occasion of Filacept. On these, scaled-down versions of the 1949 stamps are portrayed.

In 1950, Escher's good

relationship with Enschedé printers, which also donated reams of paper to him several times, resulted in a commission for the design of bank notes in denominations of Fl 10, Fl 25, Fl 50 and Fl 100. He produced attractive drawings that were very characteristic of the Escher style. They turned out to be unsuitable for their purpose. From the approximately thirty drawings Escher made for Enschedé, a selection is shown here that is different from the one presented in *The Magic Mirror of M. C. Escher* by Bruno Ernst.

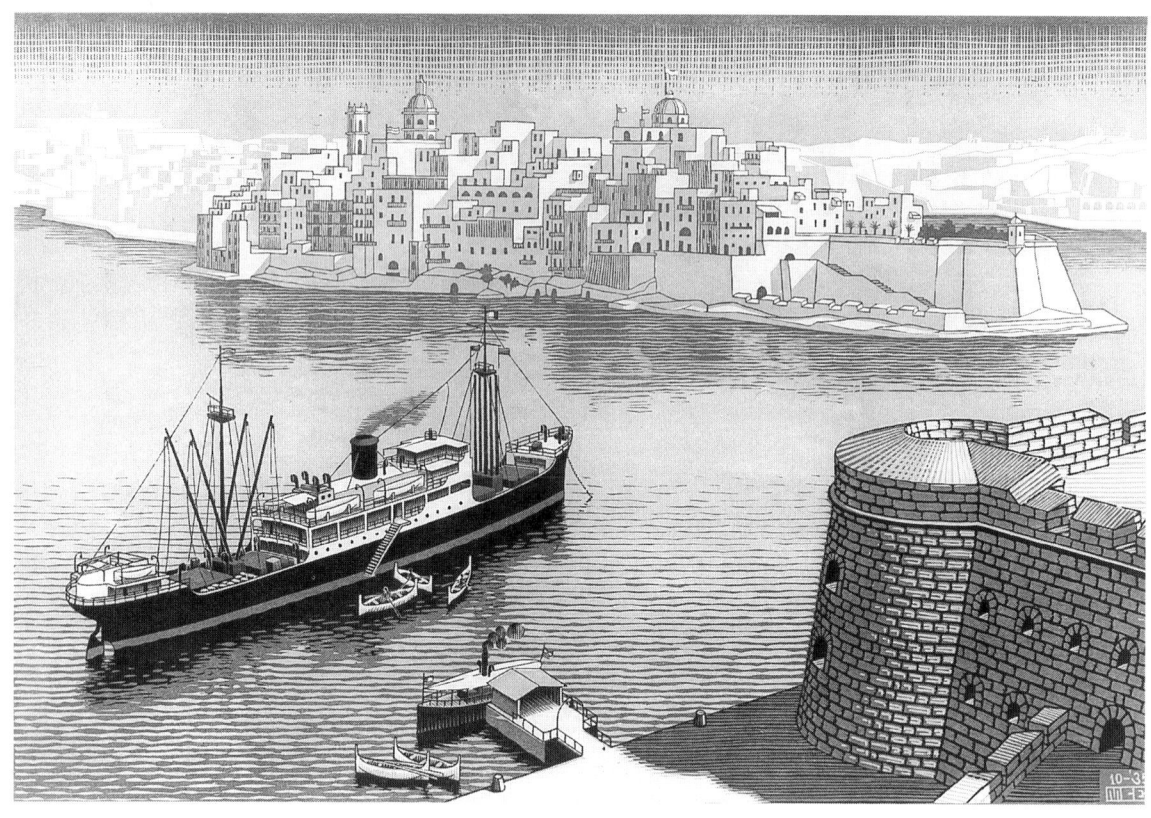

Senglea, Malta
Woodcut in three colors, 1935

Just before his departure from Italy, Escher embarked on yet another long voyage in the Mediterranean region. In May 1935, he arrived on the steamship *Verdi* at the port of Valetta, the capital of Malta. There he made a sketch of the Senglea Peninsula that would later provide the material for some important prints. The three-color woodcut shown here was done in October of the same year. In the foreground we see the *Verdi*, a ship of the Adria Company. To the right is the bastionlike building housing the customs office, which has since been demolished. Behind it is Senglea, one of the peninsulas that jut out into the port of Valetta.

29

★

30

★

★

★

★

★

★

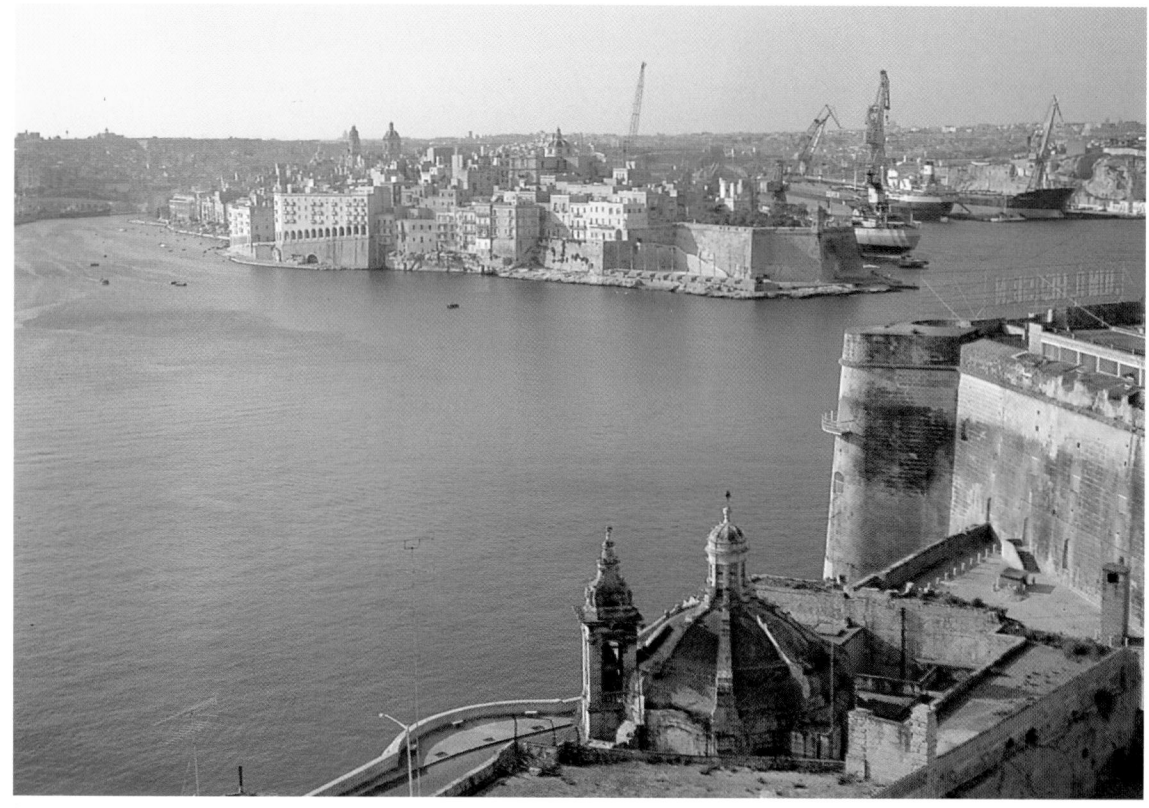

Color Photograph of Senglea

It cost me no small effort to locate
the vantage point from which
Escher drew his view of Senglea.
The main reason for the difficulty
was that during World War II the
central part of Senglea was
destroyed by bombing, and it was
never rebuilt to its original
condition. Eventually I ended up
in a small seafarers' hotel on Saint
Ursula Street, where the dining
room balcony affords exactly the
same view of Senglea as the one
depicted in Escher's print. In fact,
it provides a magnificent view of
the entire port of Valetta, with its
five peninsulas and the busy
comings and goings of freight and
passenger ships.

<table>
<tr><td>1</td><td>★</td></tr>
</table>

1

★

2

★

3

★

4

★

5

★

6

★

7

★

Snow

Lithograph, 1936

In 1935, the Escher family decided
to move to Switzerland. There
were two reasons for this: Arthur,
the second son, had contracted
tuberculosis, and his physician
recommended a healthier climate
than that of Rome. It was not
necessary to leave Italy to find
such a climate, but the political
climate under the Fascist regime
was becoming unacceptable to
Escher; George, the oldest son,
who was nine at the time, was
forced to wear the Balilla uniform
of the Fascist youth in school. So
the family moved to the Swiss
town of Chateau d'Oex. They did
not stay long, however. The two
winters in "that awful misery of
white snow," as Escher called it,
were a mental torment for him.
Fortunately, this period was
interrupted by a beautiful voyage
by ship through the Mediterranean
region and business trips to the
Netherlands.

Escher was not at all inspired by
the Swiss landscape. He made only
one lithograph there, portraying a
farmer's barn, and he did not like
it. But the children enjoyed
themselves enormously in the
snow, and George could not
understand his father's dislike. He
later wrote to C. V. S. Roosevelt: "I
also liked the lithograph of the
barn at a couple of hundred yards
from our house. Its simplicity
moved me and I saw in it many of
the things that made me happy in
our new surroundings: the
unspoiled, smooth uniformity of
the snowy landscape and the cozy,
isolated life on a farm."

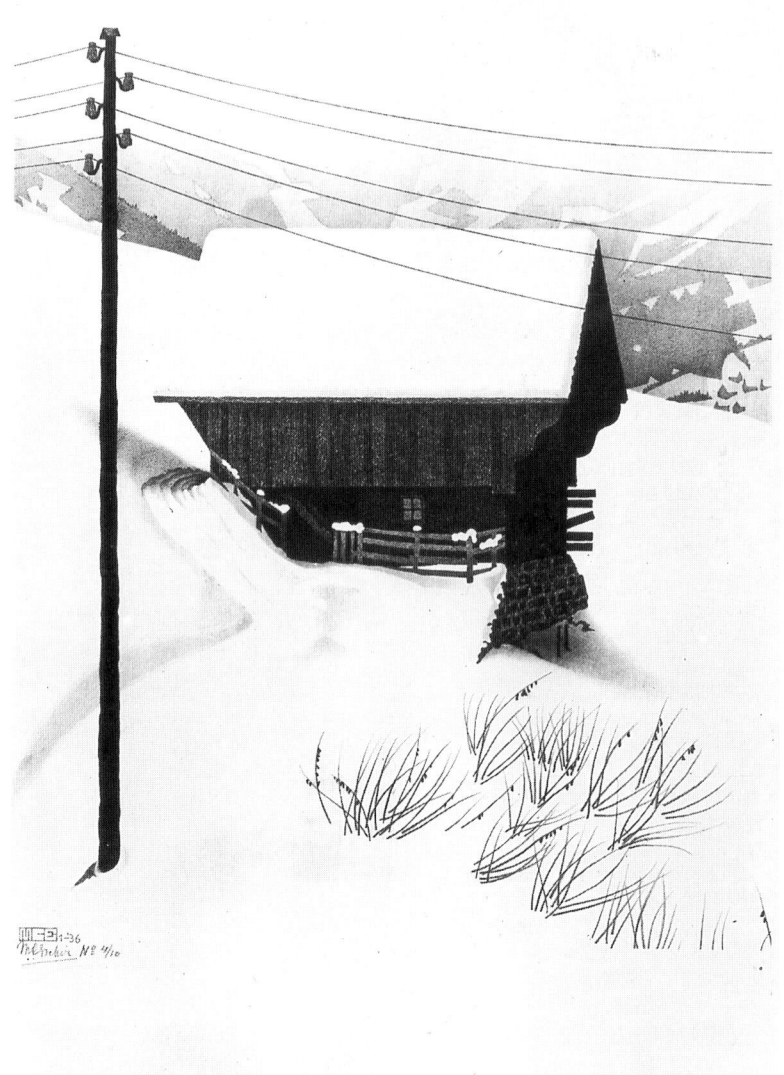

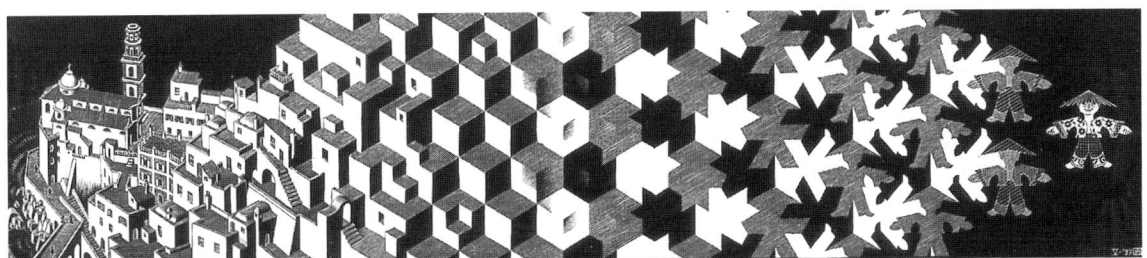

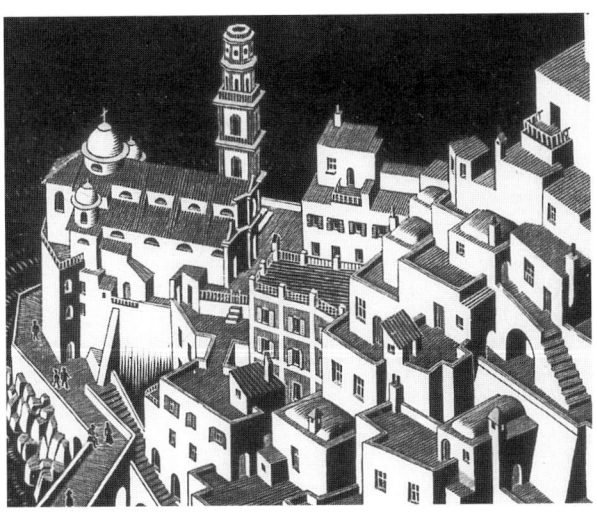

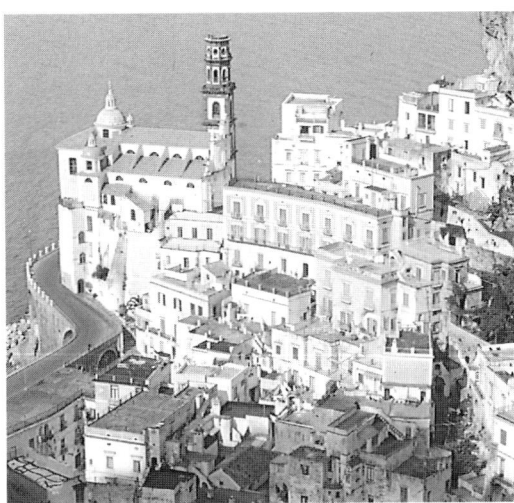

Metamorphosis I
Woodcut, 1937
Photograph of Atrani *(1974)*

Metamorphosis I, created in 1937,
clearly marked a new phase in
Escher's work. The left side of the
woodcut portrays a small area of
reality—the town of Atrani on the
coast of Amalfi. Escher had made
many drawings of it and a
lithograph as well. Farther to the
right, the blocks of houses
gradually change into a closed field
of cubes until these in turn change
into a periodic pattern of little
Chinese dolls filling up the plane.
Escher's father was not very
excited about this woodcut. He
found it puzzling and wondered
what its symbolic meaning could
be. On one of my travels, during
which I visited the places where
Escher had roamed making his
drawings, I took the photograph
shown on this page from the same
vantage point from which Escher

drew Atrani. The woodcut itself is
a faithful reproduction.

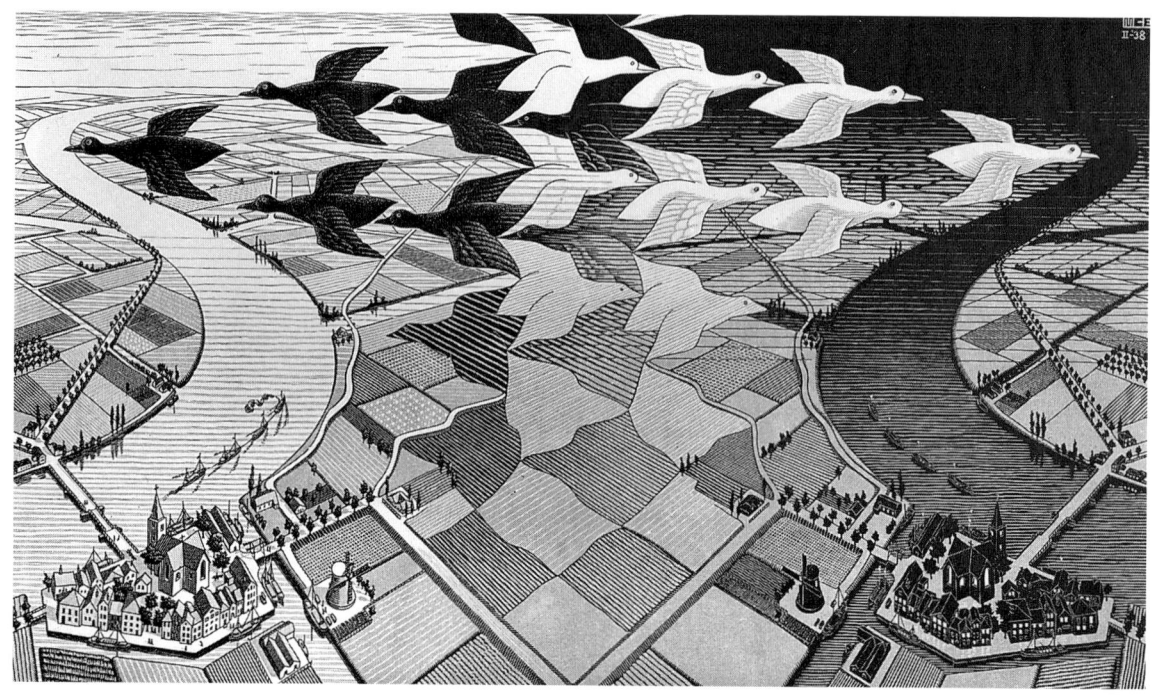

Day and Night
Woodcut in two colors, 1938

Day and Night is without a doubt the most beautiful print Escher produced in the beginning of his new period. From the bottom toward the top of the print, its rectangular fields gradually change into white and black birds. The white birds fly toward the side of the print that depicts night, and the black ones fly toward the daytime side. The visual elements are typically Dutch: a small riverside town, a steeped church, a windmill. At first, Escher's "new style" was not quite appreciated. One of the first to recognize its special character was a journalist named 's Gravesande, who wrote article after article praising it. He even published his articles in the form of a small book in May 1940 titled *M. C. Escher en zijn experimenten: Een uitzonderlijk graficus (M. C. Escher and His Experiments: An Exceptional Graphic Artist)*. **Day and Night** became one of Escher's most

requested prints, and he had to continually print new editions of it.

8   ⋆

9   ⋆

10   ⋆

11   ⋆

12   ⋆

13   ⋆

14   ⋆

May

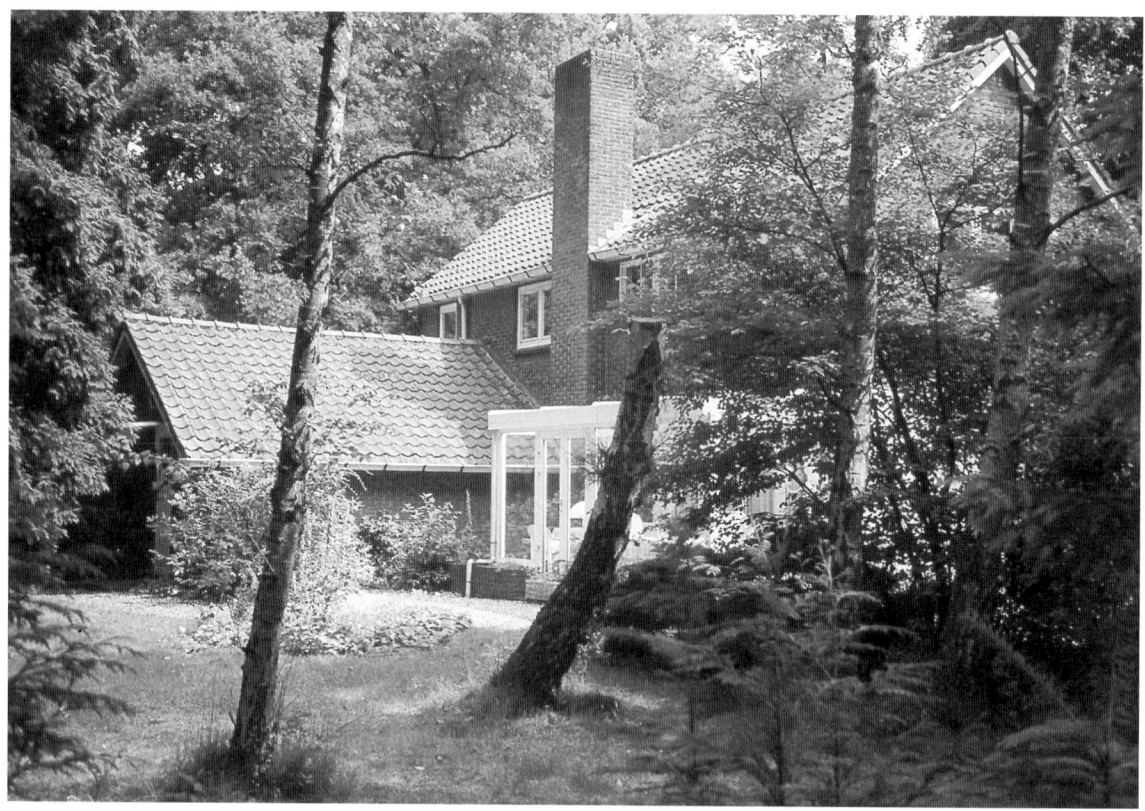

Photograph of Escher's House in Baarn at van Heemstralaan 28

In 1937, the Escher family moved to Ukkel, near Brussels, where the third son, Jan, was born in 1938. When Brussels was occupied by the Germans on May 17, 1940, Escher chose to move to the Netherlands. He rented a house at Nicolaas Beetslaan 20 in Baarn, and the family moved in on February 20, 1941. In 1954, he had a house built at van Heemstralaan in accordance with his own ideas, including a large studio with a favorable exposure. The house was ready early in 1955, and the family moved in. Much to his surprise, Escher received a royal honor on April 30 (the Queen's birthday) of that same year. He was not very excited about it and wrote Arthur: "There is one thing they will never be able to make me do, and that is to wear a decoration on my chest . . . sometimes I see these important gentlemen . . . with their medals on their chests while their carefully composed posture and courteously condescending smile clearly indicate the difference that exists between them and the sad, anonymous masses without medals."

1941	Escher settles in the Netherlands (Baarn).
1954	International Mathematicians Congress convenes in Amsterdam; it contributes to Escher becoming a well-known personality.
1959	Escher's book *Grafiek en Tekeningen M. C. Escher (The Graphic Work of M. C. Escher)* is published. It presents a summary of his work until 1959.
1965	Receives the Culture Award of the City of Hilversum.
1968	A large overview exhibition is held in the Stedelijk Museum of The Hague.
1970	Escher moves into the Rosa Spier Home.
1972	Dies on March 27 in the Diaconessenhuis Hospital in Hilversum.

15   ★

16   ★

17   ★

18   ★

19   ★

20   ★

21   ★

May

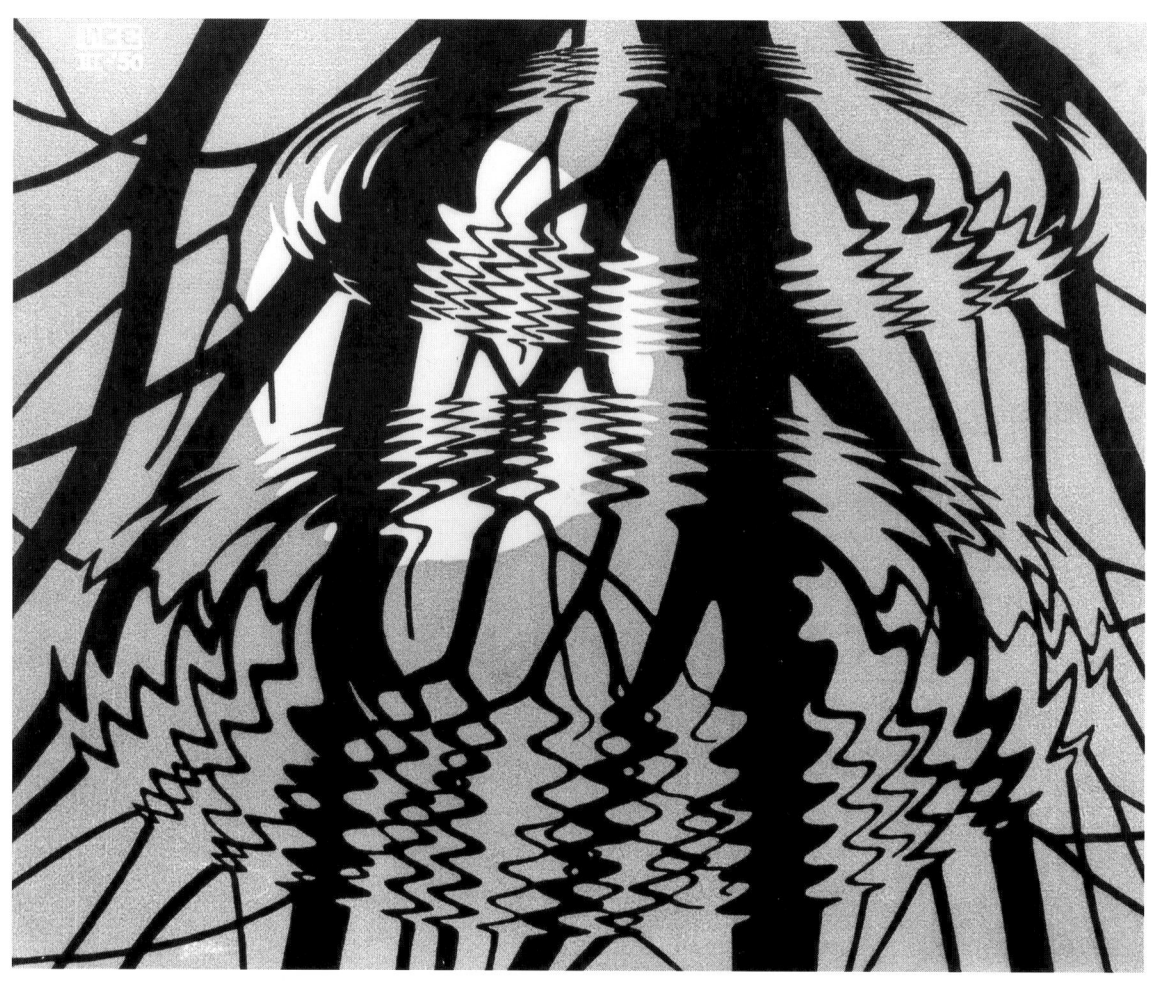

Rippled Surface
Linocut in two colors, 1950

Two or more impenetrable items cannot be present in the same place at the same time. Escher was fascinated by the fact that he was able to make them both be there when he created an image of the two items. A number of his prints deal with this theme, generally with the help of reflections. Sometimes he found the entire scene ready and waiting for him in his surroundings, as shown by *Rippled Surface* (1950), *Puddle* (1952) and *Three Worlds* (1955). The visual elements in these prints are thoroughly Dutch, a fact that distinguishes them from many others in which he returned to sketches from his Italian period. In the two-color linocut *Rippled Surface*, we see a web of bare tree branches, the sun and the ripplings on the surface of the water, all on the same plane. Escher spent considerable effort in accurately reproducing, to the extent possible, the reflections along the front edges of the two circular waves spreading in the water. This is one of the few linocuts made by Escher. He once remarked: "When I see this print hanging in my son's house in Denmark, I really think it is beautiful."

22   ✷

23   ✷

24   ✷

25   ✷

26   ✷

27   ✷

28   ✷

May

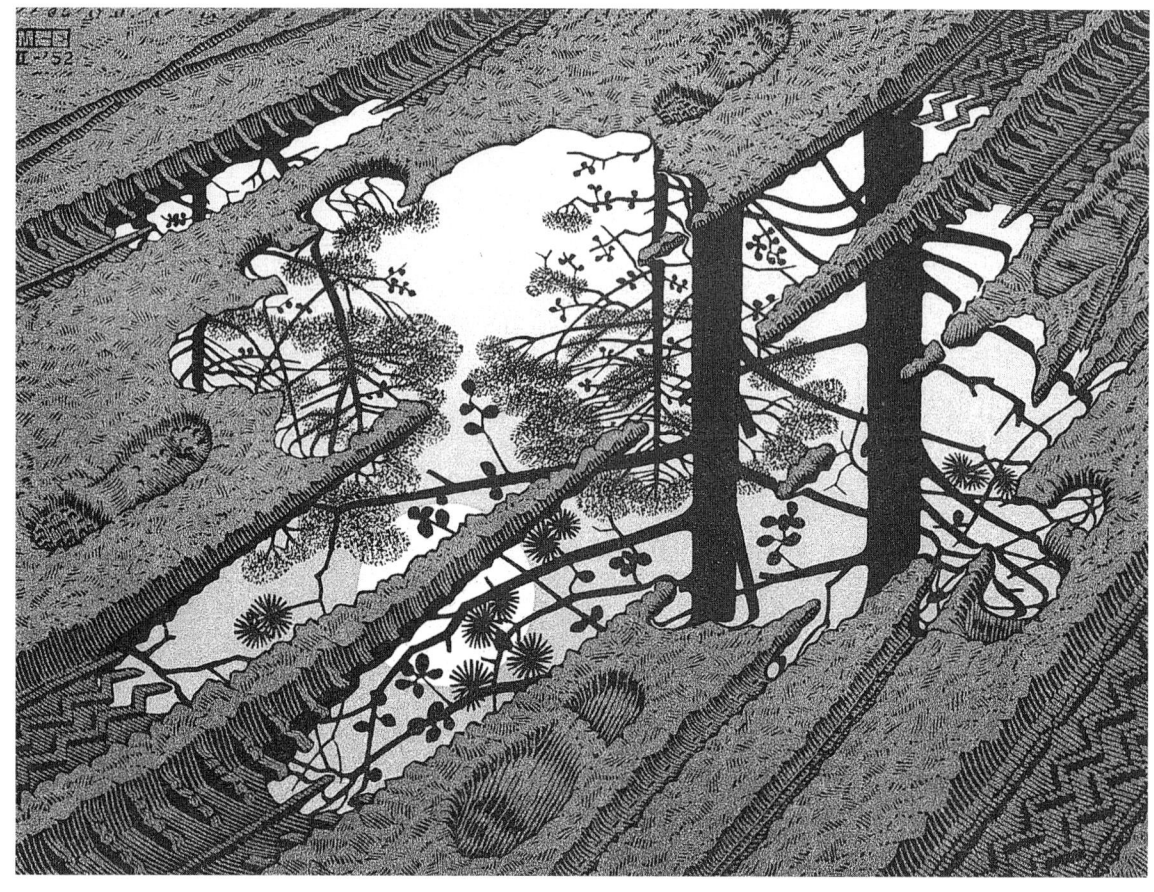

Puddle
Woodcut in three colors, 1952

The three-color woodcut titled
Puddle has the same theme as
Rippled Surface: different worlds
penetrating each other. The
muddy ground is emphatically
present in the tracks of car tires,
bicycle tires and shoe soles. The
sky, the trees and the sun are
reflected in the puddle. One could
even say that even though Escher
gave no indication of it, the
dimension of time has been
captured in the print. The tracks in
the mud are the relics of events
that took place before the point in
time that is captured in the print.

29   ⋆

30   ⋆

31   ⋆

⋆

⋆

⋆

⋆

Three Worlds
Lithograph, 1955

The idea of representing several worlds as they weave through one another continued to intrigue Escher. In *1955*, he produced the beautiful lithograph *Three Worlds*. Whereas *Rippled Surface* evokes a wintry scene with its bare trees and pale sun disk, *Three Worlds* is a typical autumn print. We see the trees of the "world of the sky" reflected in the still surface of the water, which, in its turn, is denoted by the fallen leaves that float on it. The fish marks the presence of the underwater world. "In the woods in Baarn, I walked across a little bridge and saw the scene," Escher commented. " I must make a print of this,' I thought. The title came to mind the moment I saw it. I went home and began drawing at once." This sober print reveals and at the same time conceals Escher's intention. Only the title, *Three Worlds*, plainly states the theme.

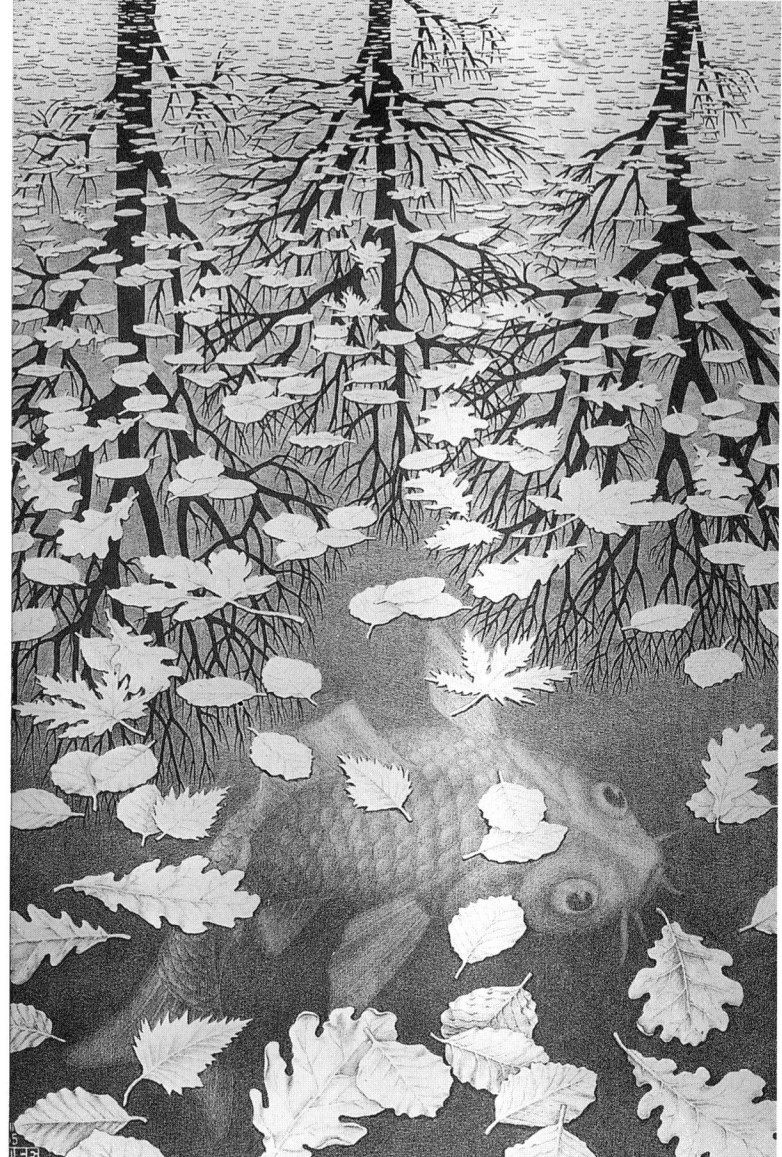

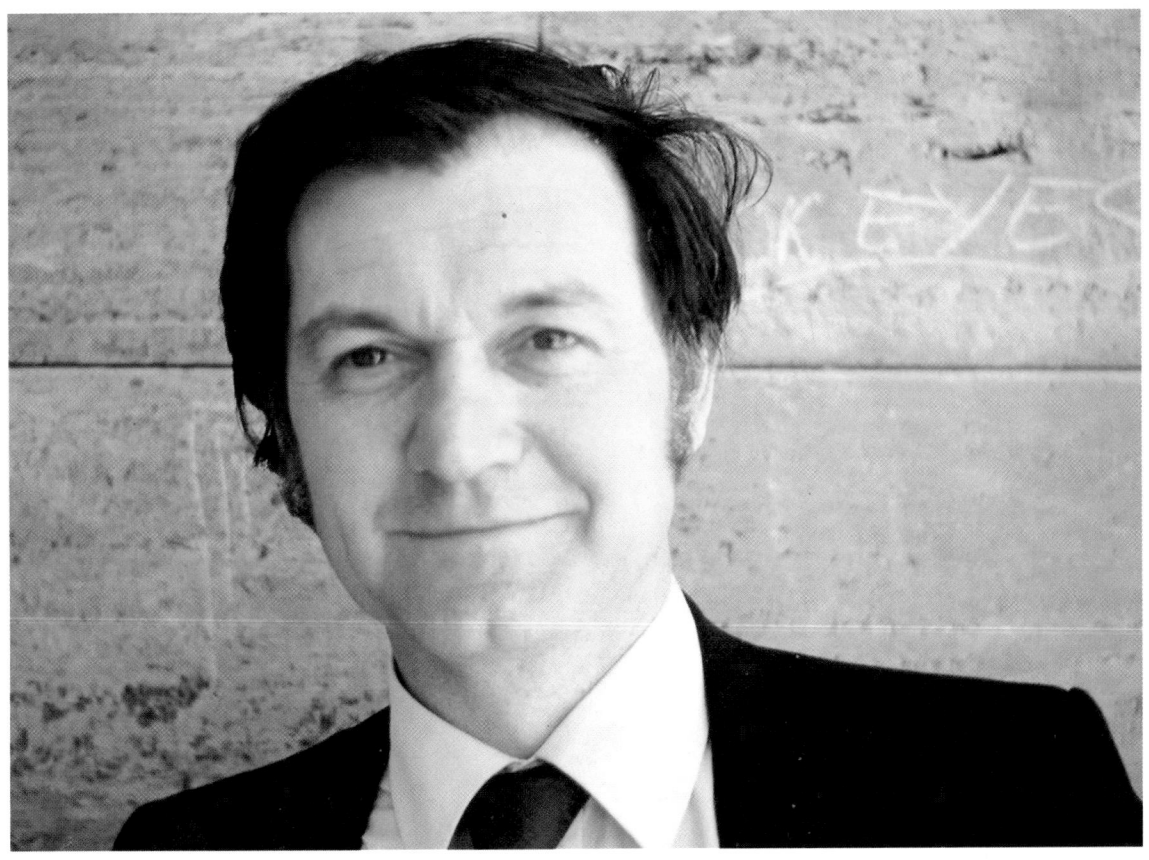

Photograph of Roger Penrose
(Rome, 1985)

In 1954, the International Mathematicians Congress was held in Amsterdam. In connection with it, the organizers presented an exhibition of Escher's work in the Stedelijk Museum in The Hague and invited him to give a lecture. Roger Penrose, a physicist and cosmologist who has since become renowned, attended this conference as a student and also visited the exhibition. "I remember that I came completely under the spell of this work, which I was seeing for the first time," Penrose recalls. "On the trip back to England, I decided to produce something 'impossible' myself . . . and eventually I arrived at the 'impossible triangle,' which in my opinion represented the impossibility that I wanted to portray in its purest form." Although the exhibition included many peculiar works by Escher, there were none that we would today call "impossible" figures.

Escher's first impossible figure was the cuboid that he worked into his print **Belvédère;** this print was produced only in 1958 (see page 24). Penrose's work was to inspire Escher to produce two important lithographs.

Ascending and Descending
Lithograph, 1960

Penrose's father, also very interested in the possibility of making truly impossible figures, invented the "impossible staircase." Together, father and son wrote an article for the *Journal of Psychology*, which was published in 1958. At the end of 1959, one of Escher's customers sent him the article, and Escher became thoroughly fascinated by this staircase without end. In the beginning of 1960, he enthusiastically wrote his son Arthur: "I am busy designing a new print that features a staircase that continuously ascends or descends, whichever way you want to go. Going around, this should normally be a spiral structure. But not in my case. It is a closed ring-shaped structure, like a snake biting itself in the tail. Still, it can be drawn correctly in accordance with perspective, showing every step higher or lower than the previous one. . . . Oh yes, we keep on climbing; we imagine that we are climbing; every step is almost eight inches high, terribly tiring, and where does it get us? Nowhere; we do not get one step farther or higher."

Escher wrote to the Penroses: "Your figures 3 and 4, Continuous Staircase, were totally new to me, and I was so impressed with the idea that it recently inspired me to make a new print. I would like to send you an original copy as a token of my respect."

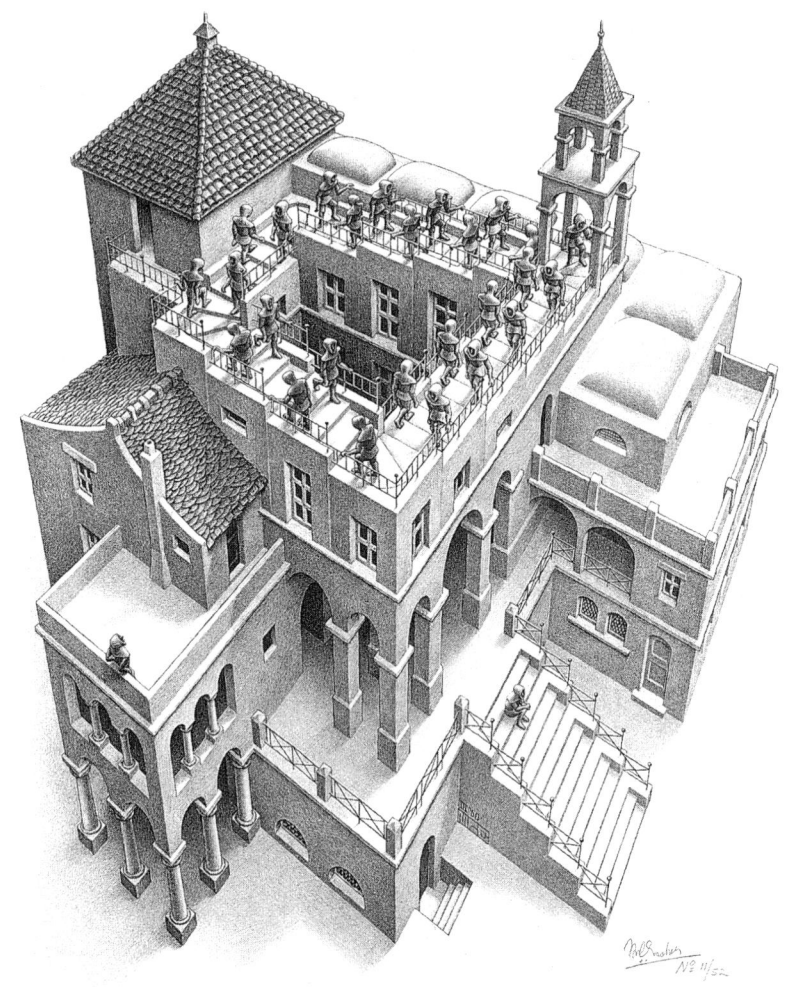

1   ⋆

2   ⋆

3   ⋆

4   ⋆

5   ⋆

6   ⋆

7   ⋆

June

8   ⋆

9   ⋆

10   ⋆

11   ⋆

12   ⋆

13   ⋆

14   ⋆

June

15   *

16   *

17   *

18   *

19   *

20   *

21   *

June

| 22 | | ⋆ |

| 23 | | ⋆ |

| 24 | | ⋆ |

| 25 | | ⋆ |

| 26 | | ⋆ |

| 27 | | ⋆ |

| 28 | | ⋆ |

June

Waterfall
Lithograph, 1961

The lithograph **Waterfall** was ready in October 1961, and Escher sent one of the first prints to Penrose on December 1, writing: "I owe you something again. I could not stop thinking about your exciting 'triangle.' The result is a lithograph, which I have just completed. I am sending you a print of it today so as to unburden my conscience. The two polyhedrons on the towers have no symbolic meaning whatsoever. I put them there only because I liked them."

The building is located somewhere near Amalfi and it could constitute a mechanism in perpetual motion created to keep the hammers of a small paper factory busy. The water flows downward continuously, but it still ends up at the top, from whence it cascades down like a waterfall onto the wheel.

The nucleus of the image consists of three impossible triangles that are linked together. It is one of the best-loved Escher prints, probably because it very emphatically gives us the sensation of seeing the impossible.

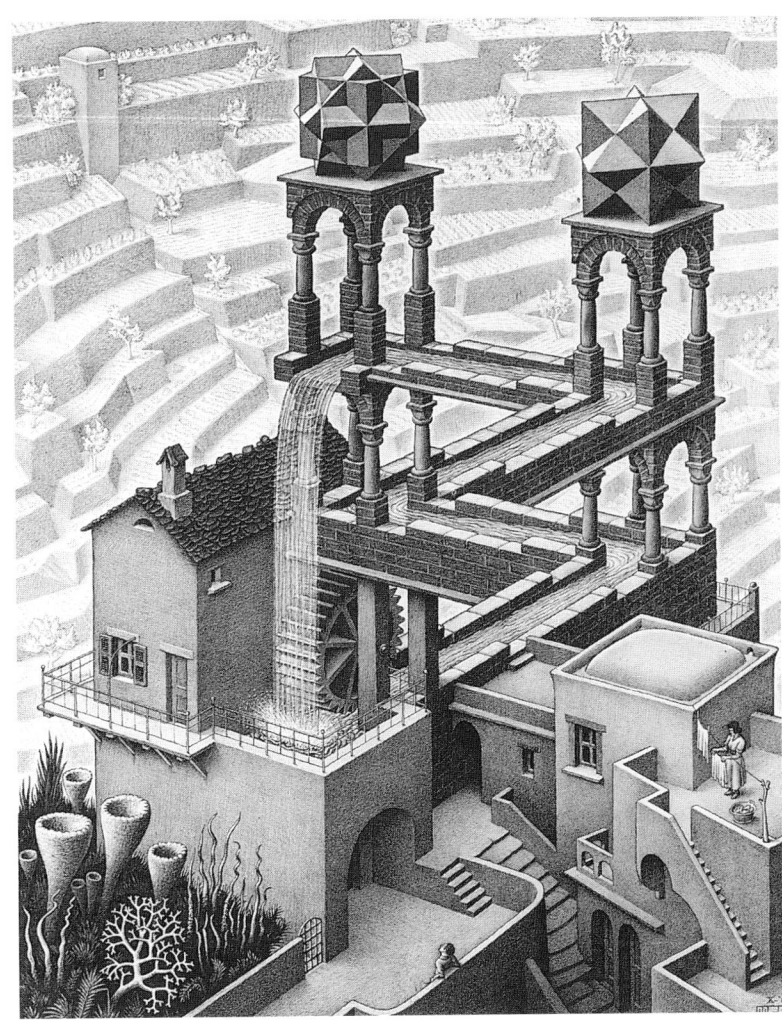

June

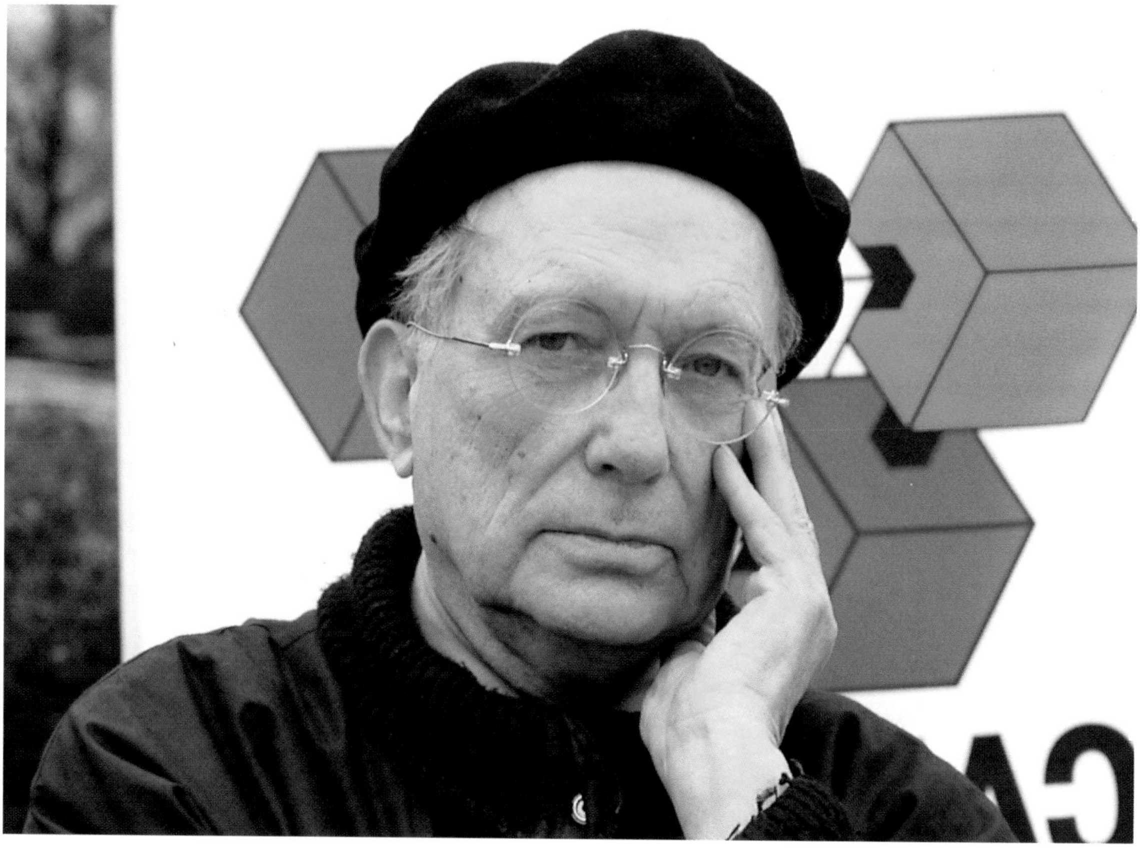

Photograph of Oscar Reutersvärd

In a 1960 letter to Roger Penrose, Escher wrote: "If you should have other published articles with accurate drawings about impossible objects or related subjects, or if you should know about such articles, I would be very much obliged to you if you could provide me information about these." So Escher was looking for new structures even though he had not yet exhausted the possibilities of the three with which he was familiar—the cuboid, the triangle and the staircase. But Escher generally worked to produce only an example: once he had given expression to a certain idea, he was through with it.

Neither the elder nor the younger Penrose had any new ideas for impossible figures. However, such figures did exist in abundance! Oscar Reutersvärd, a Swedish art historian, had unintentionally drawn the first "impossible figure" in 1934. By 1960 he had found hundreds of them. In 1982 the Swedish postal service issued a series of stamps with some of Reutersvärd's "impossible figures." How could it be that Escher and Reutersvärd did not know each other? Reutersvärd told me that he had written to Escher in 1962, 1964 and 1965 after he saw reproductions of **Ascending and Descending** and **Waterfall**. It remains a mystery why Escher did not answer these letters from an admirer.

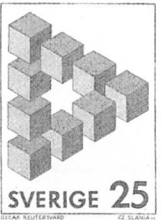
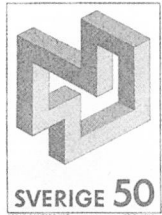

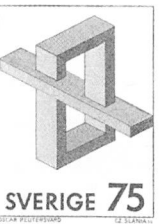

1

⋆

2

⋆

3

⋆

4

⋆

5

⋆

6

⋆

7

⋆

Balcony
Lithograph, 1945

In 1945, Escher came across the following problem: What happens if I allow a plane to swell up somewhere in the middle? Where would the part of the plane that gets pushed away end up? It was actually a simple problem, which was quickly demonstrated by a sketch on graph paper. The small squares in the area around the swelling were squeezed together in a systematic manner. Escher was curious to see what a drawing would look like if he should apply this kind of transformation to it. So he looked through his sketchbooks for a suitable subject. He chose his sketch of Senglea because it featured so many small cubelike elements—that is, the blocks of houses. Escher focused on a balcony, which became the considerably enlarged central part of the lithograph. If we compare **Balcony** with the woodcut **Senglea** (page 52), which he had produced ten years earlier, we can see that he transferred the central part of this latter print rather accurately.

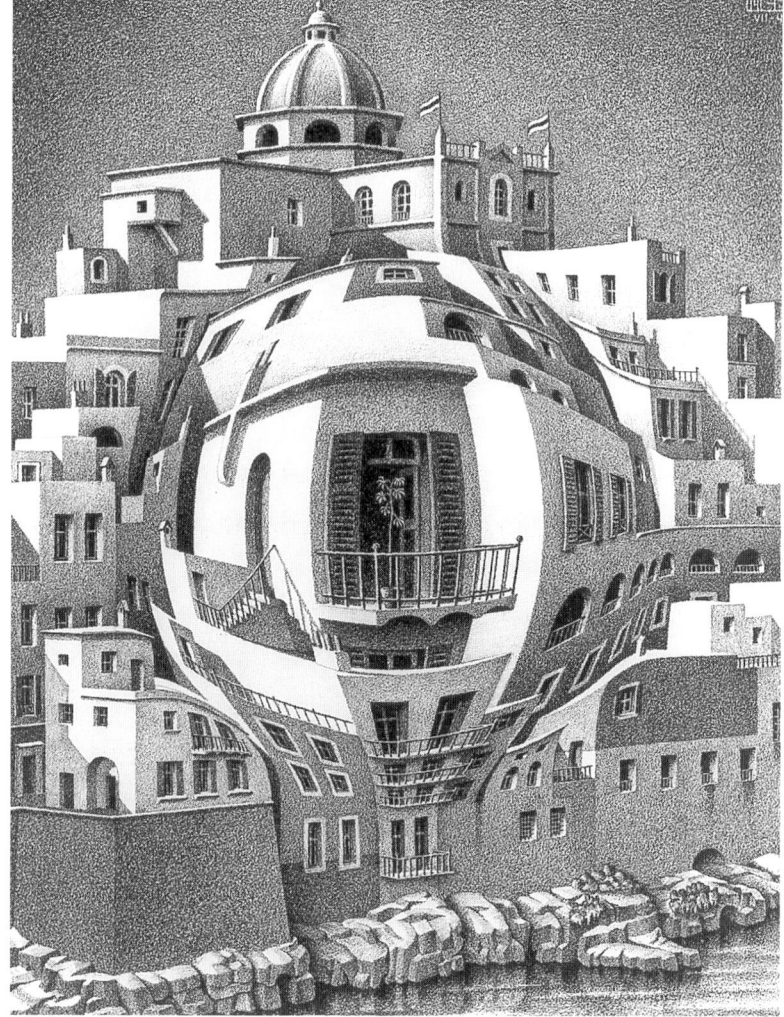

8

★

9

★

10

★

11

★

12

★

13

★

14

★

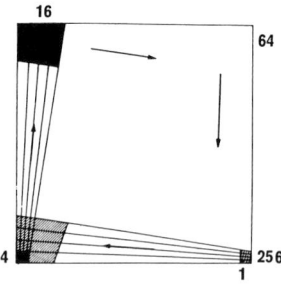

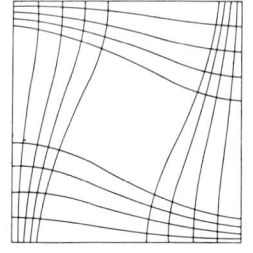

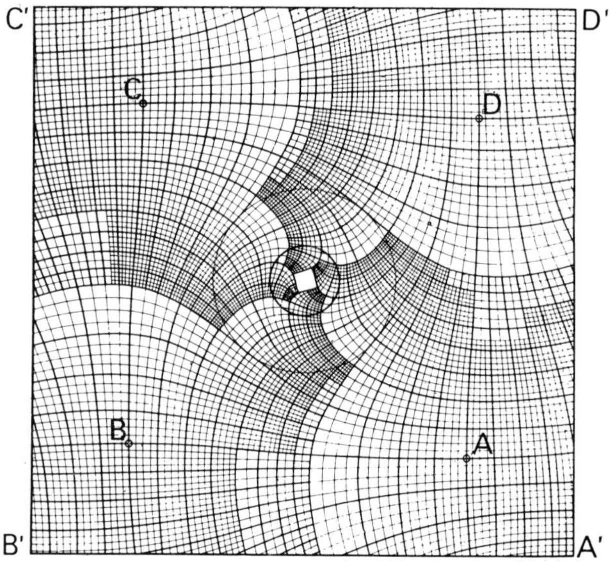

Preliminary Study for *Print Gallery*

Eleven years after Escher used a sketch of Senglea on the island of Malta to embellish his lithograph ***Balcony,*** he posed a much more difficult problem related to the deformation of the plane. Again he used the Senglea sketch, but this time more completely and ingeniously. In ***Balcony,*** the issue was the swelling up of a plane starting out in the center. Here, the issue is a ring-shaped swelling.

We first need to imagine a square drawing plane, denoted as ABCD, like the one pictured above. We start out with a small square that has one of its corners in A; then we proceed to B. Meanwhile we let the small square slowly grow until it has become four times as large by the time we get to B. From B, we go upward toward C while letting the square again become four times as large. Going around through D we return to A, and the original square has by now become 256 times as large. Can something like this be drawn? What happens to the entire drawing plane? What happens outside the drawing plane—for example, the plane enclosed by A'B'C'D'? It is definitely not a simple problem,

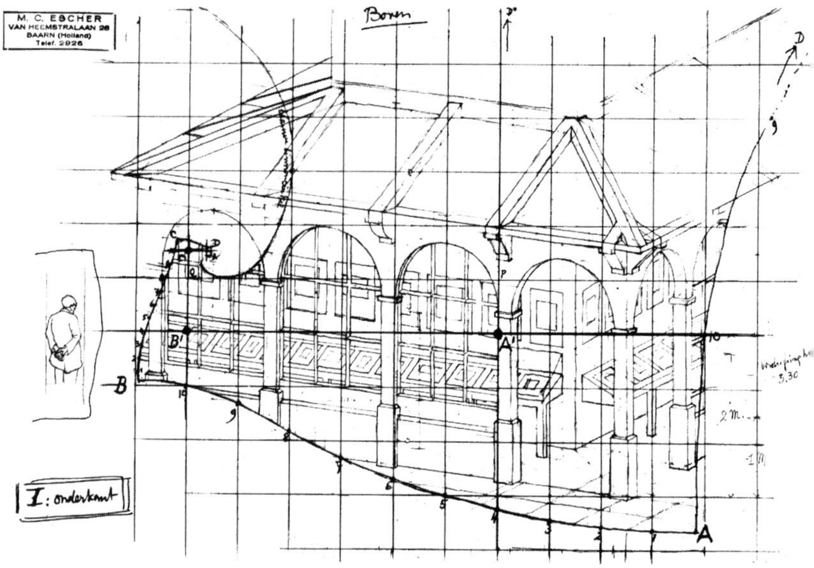

but Escher managed to solve it, as can be seen in this network.

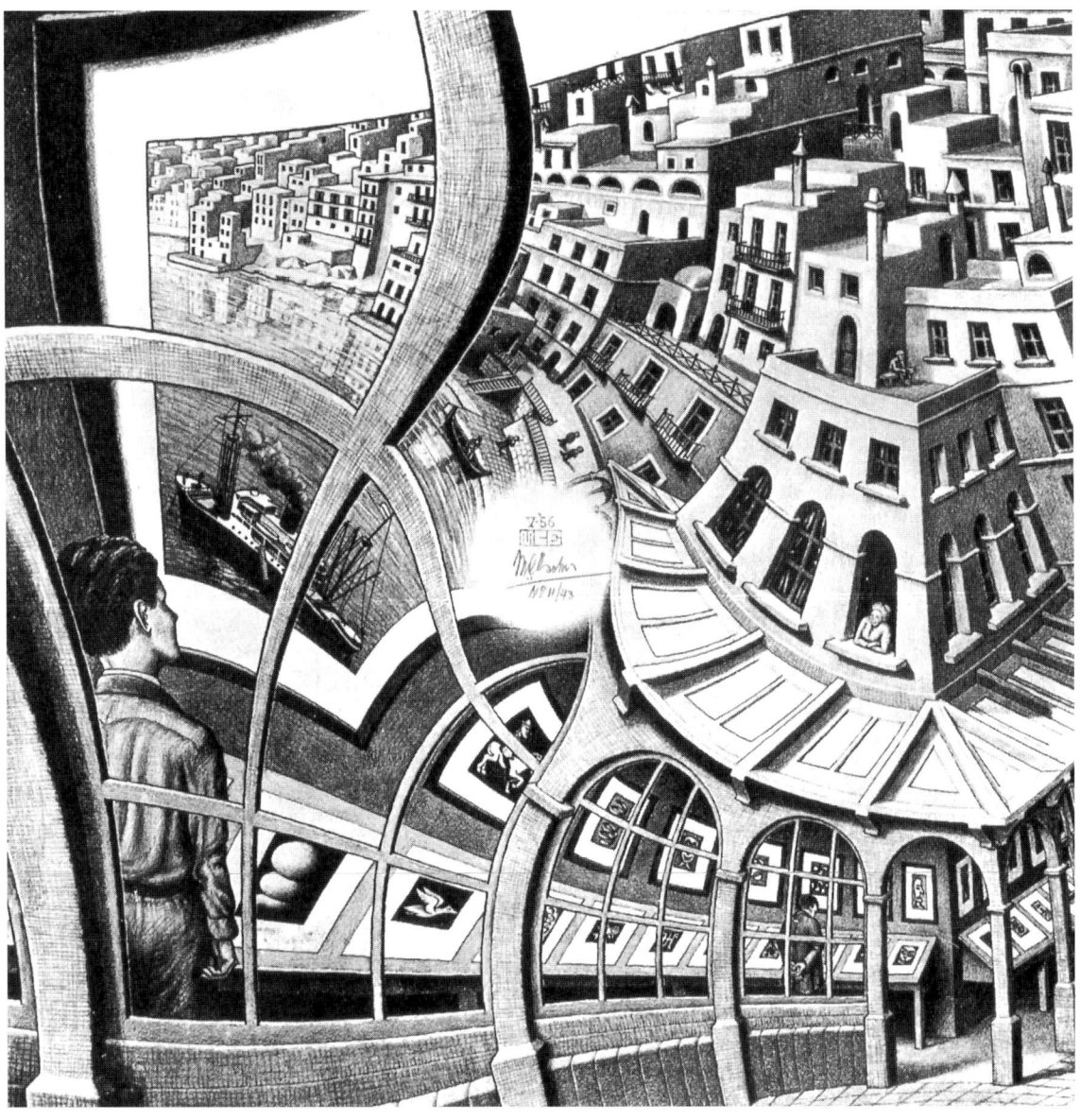

Print Gallery
Lithograph, 1956

Print Gallery is not an attractive
print. In its upper left-hand
corner, we see an annoying cross
with curving lines, which
constitutes a disturbing element.
Yet even though it is not beautiful,
it still is the cleverest print Escher
ever made. In the lower right-hand
corner, we enter a gallery where
prints are exhibited. A boy is
looking at the prints. Toward the
left, the gallery becomes gradually
larger and we again meet up with
the boy; but now he is almost four
times as big. He is looking at a
print, and it is a print we know: it
is the woodcut done in 1935 titled
Senglea. However, the print also
becomes ever larger as we proceed
toward the right. This is where the
big practical problem presented
itself for Escher: what to do with
the content of the images so as to
arrive again at the point of
departure with an enlargement of
256 times and to do this in a way
that seemed natural. The solution
is a stroke of genius. The print
gallery becomes a part of one of
the houses in the print, so we end
up inside the gallery again . . . but
it is not the same gallery as before
because this one is depicted on a
print in that gallery! The boy on
the left is depicted on a print at
which he is looking.

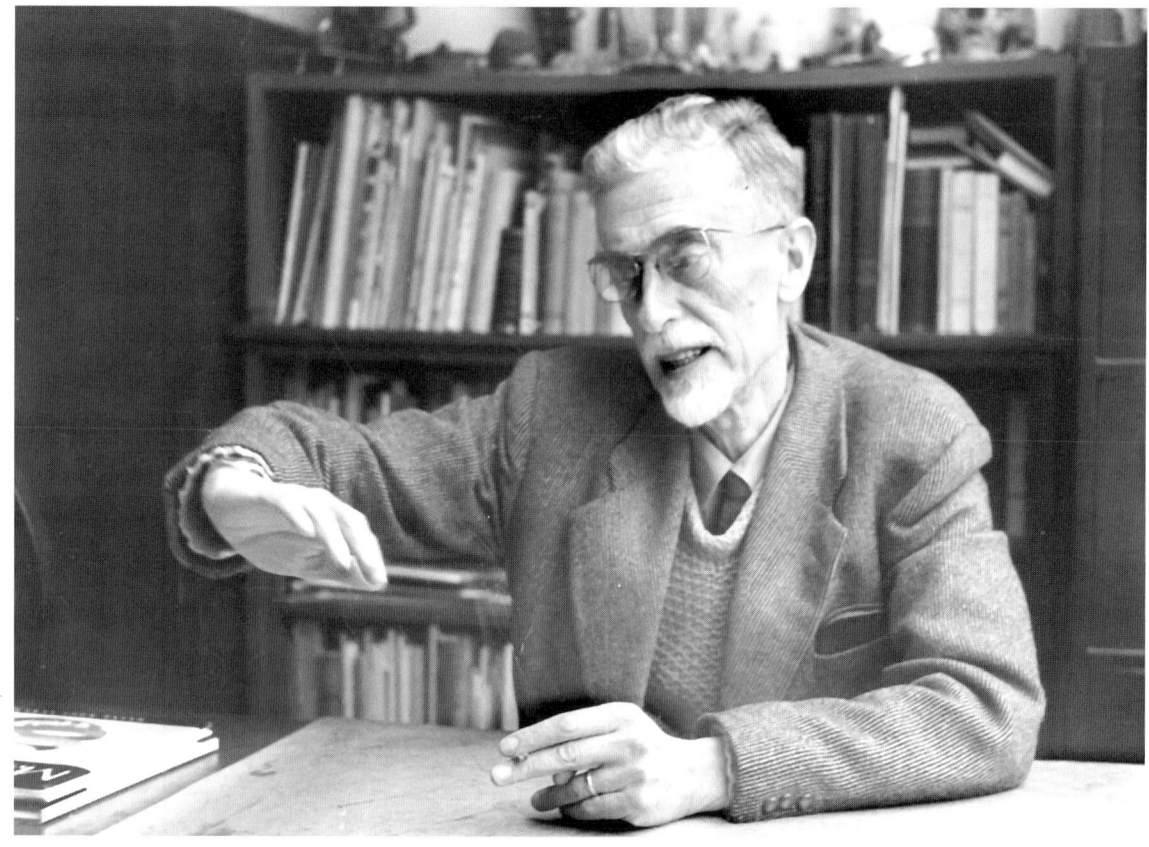

Photograph of Escher (*1956*)

In 1956, I visited Escher for the first time in his studio in Baarn. I had seen his print **High and Low** and I wanted to learn more about it. Escher considered a written explanation too cumbersome, so he invited me over for a personal conversation. He was putting the finishing touches on **Print Gallery** and I criticized the ugly cross in the upper left-hand corner.

When I got home, I wrote him suggesting that he might be able to camouflage the cross by letting a clematis climb on it. Just imagine! Escher was almost sixty, had more than earned his stripes as a graphic artist and already enjoyed considerable recognition as the creator of very unusual prints. I was thirty and a teacher of mathematics. He wrote me a letter, which I have reproduced on page 83. It is eloquent not only because it expresses his own view of his work as an artist but especially because it shows how seriously he took the criticism of a young man who hardly knew his work.

15

    *

16

    *

17

    *

18

    *

19

    *

20

    *

21

    *

22   ★

23   ★

24   ★

25   ★

26   ★

27   ★

28   ★

29

30

31

The clematis border along the "beams" on my **Print Gallery** would doubtlessly be beautiful. But those beams are meant to represent window frames. Furthermore, I had probably already spent so much energy in "thinking out the details" of this image that I was too numb to be able to better meet aesthetic requirements. I simply have to rack my brains to produce these prints. Besides, none of them was ever made for the primary purpose of creating "something beautiful." That is also the reason that I never quite feel in the right place while I am among my fellow graphic artists. *They* strive for "beauty" first and foremost (even though this concept has changed greatly since the 17th century—for them as well!), while *I*, on the other hand, focus maybe exclusively on the element of wonder, and, therefore, I also try to evoke only a sense of wonder in my viewers. Sometimes "beauty" does not come off so well.

De clematis-omranking van de „balken" op mijn prententententoonstelling zou ongetwijfeld fraai zijn. Evenwel zijn die balken bedoeld als sponningen van ruiten. Tevens heeft waarschijnlijk het „uitdenken" van zulk een voorstelling al zó veel van mijn energie geëist, dat ik te afgestompt was om beter aan aesthetische eisen te voldoen. Deze prenten (die trouwens geen van allen ooit gemaakt werden met het primaire oogmerk „iets moois" te maken) kosten mij gewoonweg hoofdbrekens. Dat is dan ook de reden, dat ik mij, te midden van mijn grafici-collega's, nooit volkomen op mijn plaats voel: zij streven, in de eerste plaats „schoonheid" na (al is dat begrip door de eeuwigjaren, ook voor hen, sinds de 17e eeuw!). Misschien streef ik wel uitsluitend verwondering na en tracht ik dus ook uitsluitend verwondering bij mijn toeschouwers te wekken. Met de „schoonheid" is het soms kwalijk gesteld.

—From a letter to the author by M. C. Escher, 1956

In this letter, Escher explained that he did not want to make something beautiful but that he wanted to transmit his own sense of wonder to his viewers. **Print Gallery**, his "ugly" print, is the strongest example of this striving.

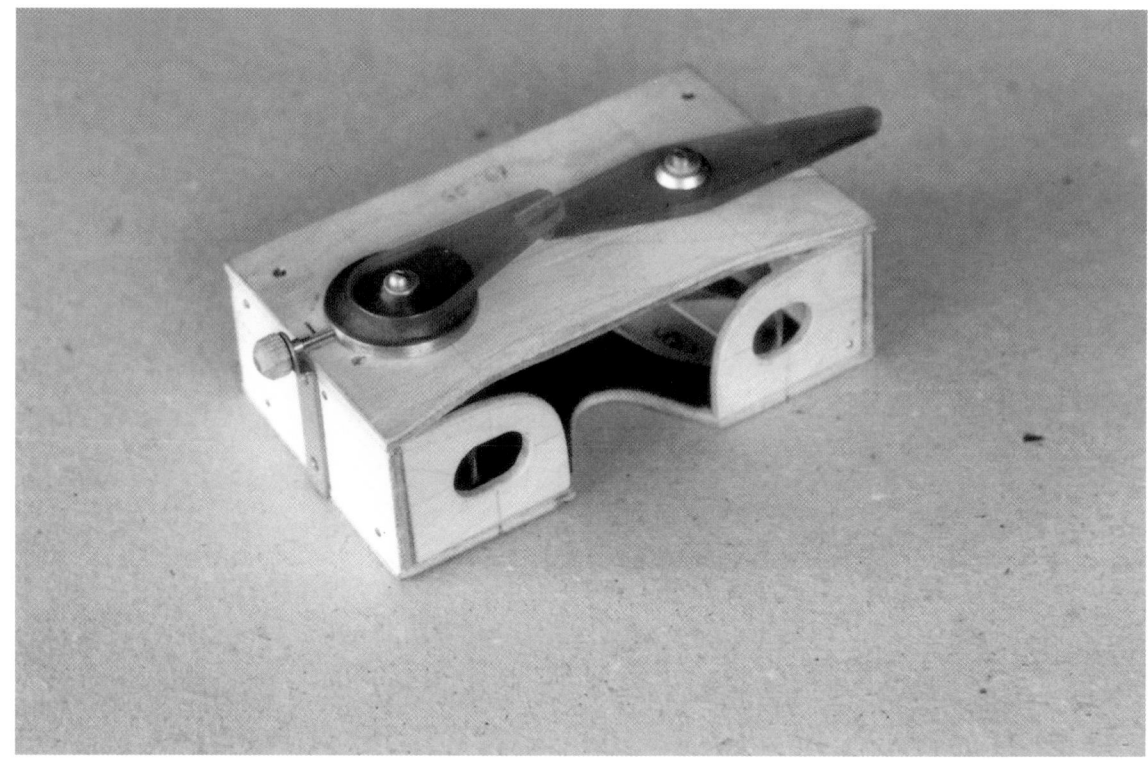

Pseudoscope
Copy of Escher's own model

After my first visit to Escher, he wrote to his son Arthur: "This time I wanted to tell you something about . . . a strange guy who suddenly one day decided to write me that my prints fascinated him, as well as the boys whom he teaches, and that he would like to come to Baarn to take a look. And so he did. He looked with great interest at my doodles on perspective and especially at my 'inversion' print titled *Convex and Concave* (which I sent you, I think), as well as at my periodic patterns for the regular division of planes.

"As we discussed the *Convex and Concave* print, he suggested a method that makes it easy to 'invert' all kinds of objects and landscapes that we happen to see. It is so amazingly stunning that I want to explain to you how you can do it. You need two good rectangular prisms. . . ." The letter continued with an extensive description of all the amazing inversions Escher had observed using this method. It was truly a new world, turned inside out. The pseudoscope that Escher himself crafted was lost. The one shown above is a copy that I had made (by Jan Kragten) at a later date.

1

★

2

★

August

3

★

4

★

5

★

6

★

7

★

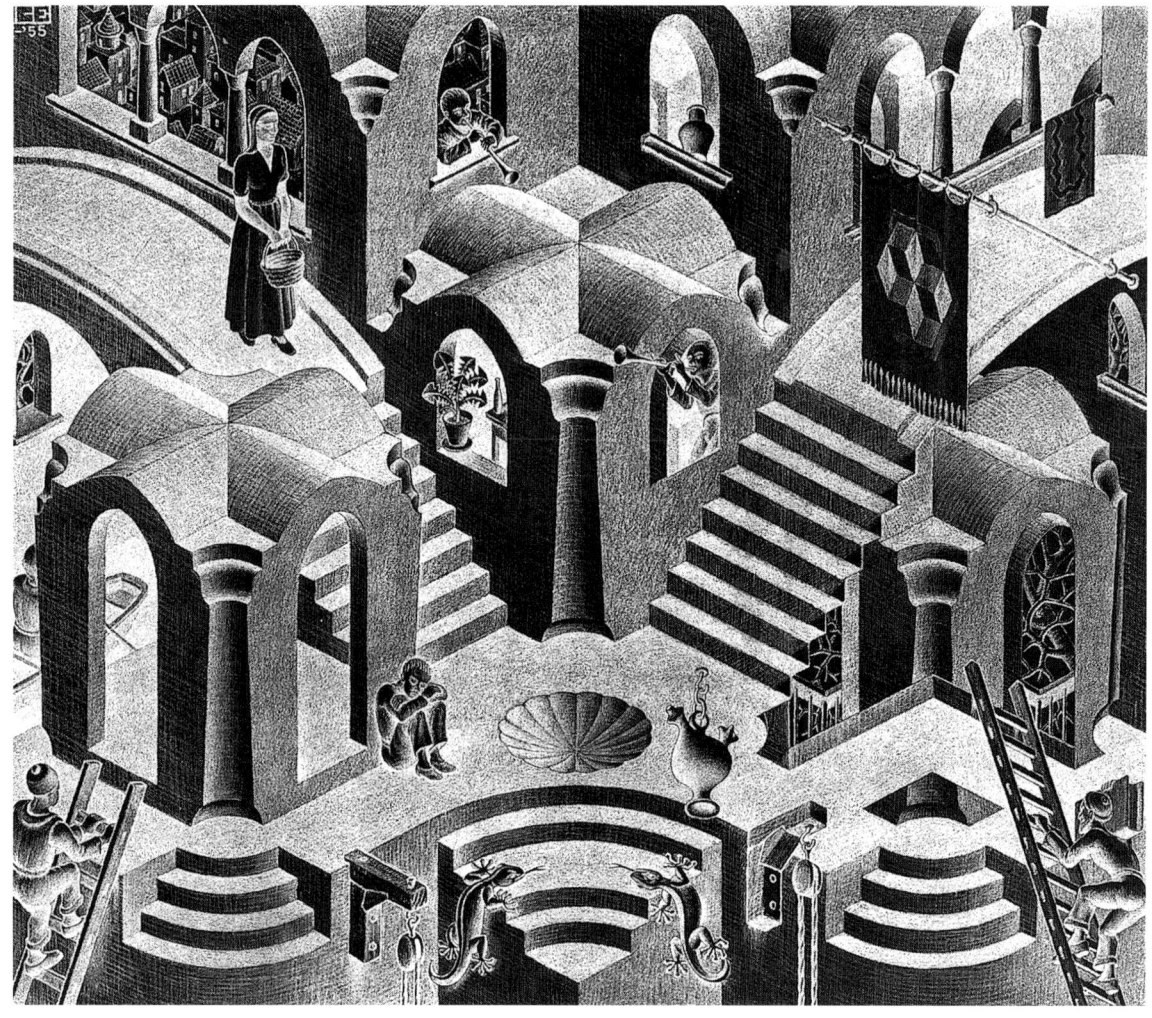

Convex and Concave
Lithograph, 1955

The German mineralogist L. A. Necker was the first to point out that when we look at the image of a cube, we can see it in two very different positions.

This is shown in the print ***Convex and Concave***. The structure shown seems to be symmetrical. On the left is a small temple in the shape of a cube. To the right is another cube at the same height, but we see it from the bottom, and we see the inside of it. In the middle, somewhat higher up than these two cubes, we see another cube.

Whether we see this last one as concave or convex depends on whether we let our eyes go from left to right (when it seems to be a small cube-shaped temple) or from right to left (when we see a hollowing out of the architecture). In the center area of the print, ambiguity and confusion prevail, which irritates some people and greatly amazes others.

8   ★

9   ★

10   ★

11   ★

12   ★

13   ★

14   ★

**Photograph of Professor
MacGillavry**
(Rome, 1985)

Icosahedral Cookie Box *(1963)*

In 1959, Escher became a member
of the Rotary Club of Baarn, and
his book *Grafiek en tekeningen
(The Graphic Work of M. C.
Escher)*, which presented an
overview of his work, was
published. But, as he wrote his son
Arthur: "The most pleasant thing,
however, that happened to me
recently was a visit by a lady,
Professor Dr. MacGillavry, who
teaches crystallography at the
University of Amsterdam. She
came with her sister-in-law, and,
from half past two until at least
half past five, the two of them
looked through my prints. They
certainly were a couple of sharp
ladies!"

Professor MacGillavry arranged
for Escher to give a lecture at the
Crystallographers Congress in
Cambridge in 1960 and arranged
for his work to be exhibited there.
It was an enormous success. One
of the outcomes was that he gave
lectures and held exhibitions in
Toronto and in Cambridge,
Massachusetts, that same year. In
addition, MacGillavry conceived
the plan to publish a book with
Escher's periodic drawings
*(Symmetry Aspects of M. C. Escher's
Periodic Drawings*, 1963).
The icosahedron (a box with
twenty regular planes) shown here
was designed by Escher in 1963 as a
promotional gift (a cookie box) for
Verblifa.

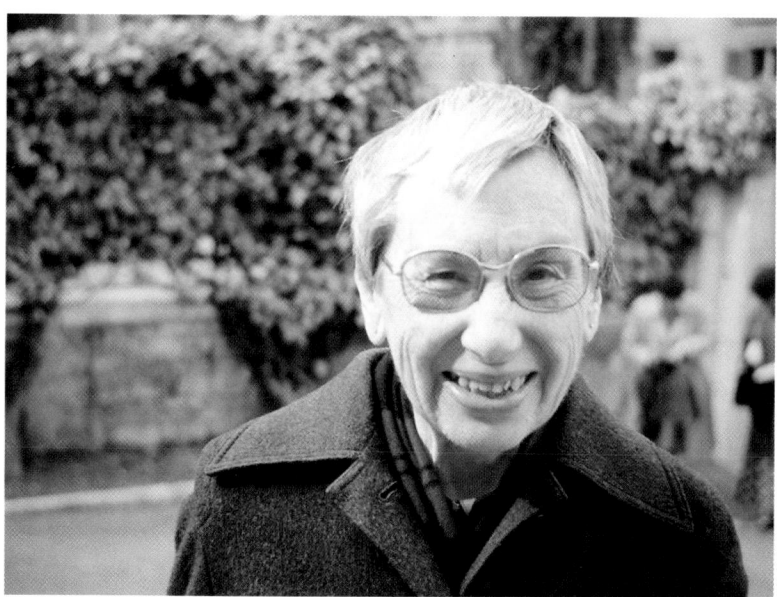

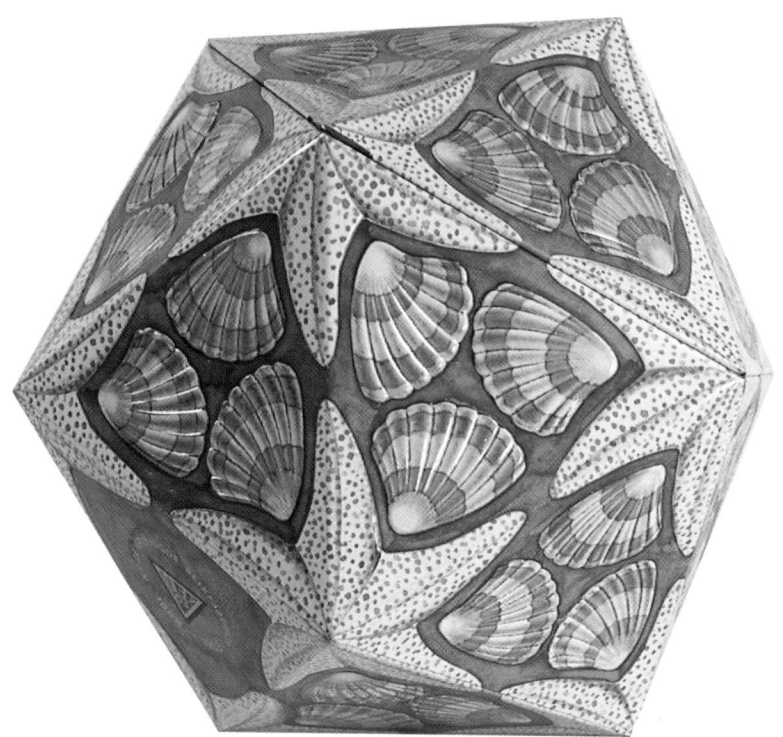

15   ★

16   ★

17   ★

18   ★

19   ★

20   ★

21   ★

August

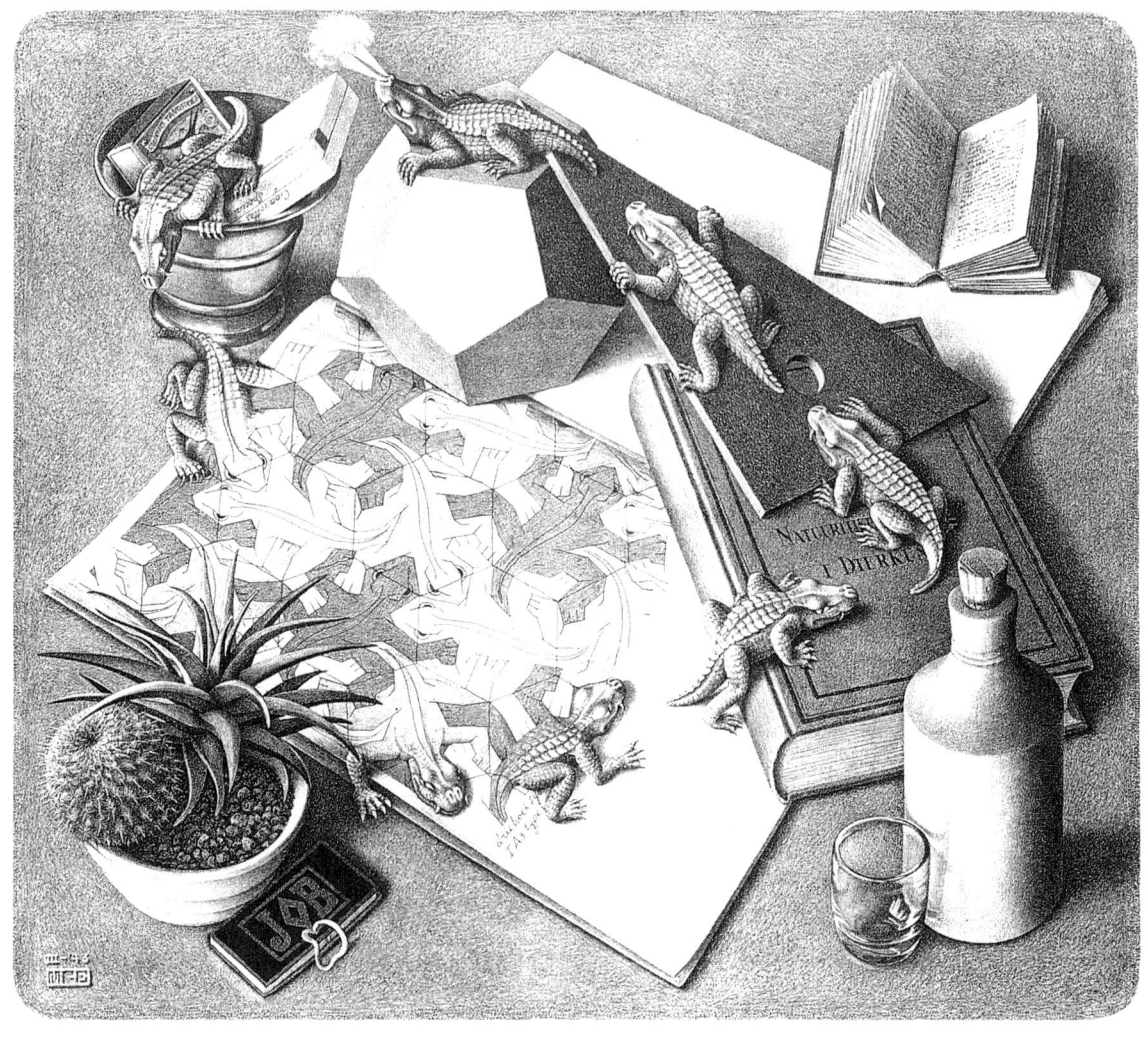

Reptiles
Lithograph, 1943

In the lithograph **Reptiles**, we see Escher's drawing pad with periodic patterns for the regular division of a plane opened up at a page filled with reptiles. They are flat, of course, since they have been drawn. But is that really logical? One reptile is crawling out of the drawing. It is flat as well, but a three-dimensional picture is being shaped in our brains and it seems a real reptile. It even goes for a walk, crawls over the zoology book and over the dodecahedron, where it spews smoke from its nostrils like a wild dragon. But it was all fiction. Drawing is fiction, a suggestion of spatiality on a plane. In the end, the reptile disappears again into the pad with the periodic drawings.

22   ★

23   ★

24   ★

25   ★

26   ★

27   ★

28   ★

August

29	*

30	*

31	*

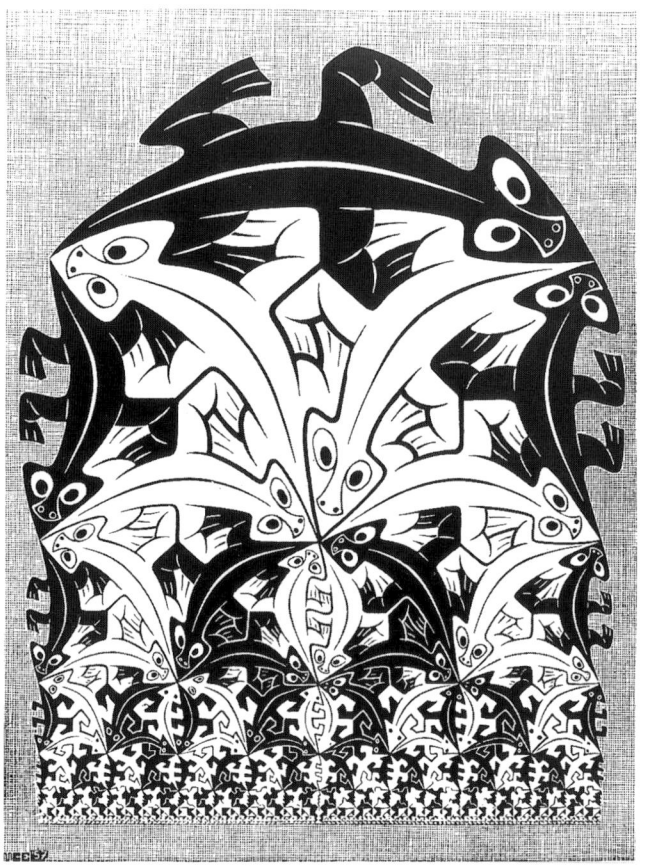

Regular Division of the Plane with Approach to Infinity

Throughout his life, Escher continued to be interested in the challenge of the regular division of planes with periodic patterns. His introduction to the splendid examples of such drawings that are found at the Alhambra, in the Spanish city of Granada, formed a strong motivation for him to systematically investigate the possibilities afforded by this technique. Escher, however, wanted to fill his planes with clearly recognizable plants, animals and people rather than using geometric motifs. In 1958, he wrote a treatise on the subject in an edition intended for bibliophiles and published by the De Roos Foundation. For this edition he also made six new woodcuts, one of which is reproduced here. To the periodic drawings of the lizards he added a second element: that of the approach to infinity. As it approaches the lower part of the print, the endlessly receding plane is systematically compressed until it becomes a visible boundary.

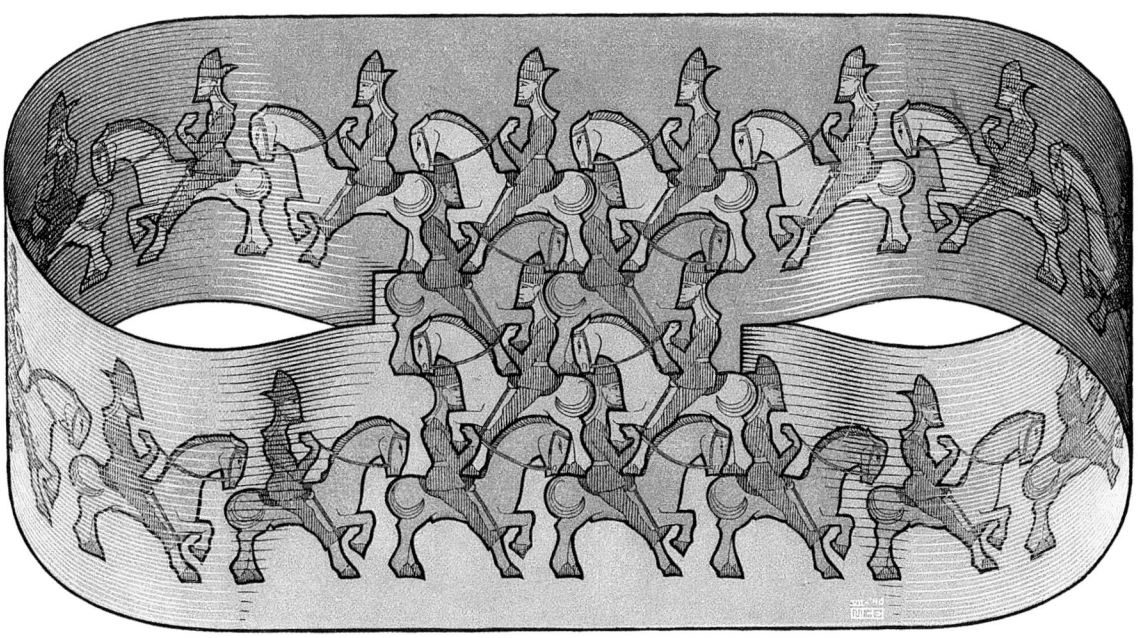

Horseman
Woodcut in three colors, 1946

Periodic patterns make up the center of this woodcut, in which the entire plane is filled with red and gray horsemen. The red riders are mirror images of the gray ones, and in a vertical direction, they have been moved over slightly with respect to one another. This arrangement is called a "glide reflection." The other happenings in this print have been aptly described by Pam Rueter, a graphic artist and colleague of Escher's, in a poem written especially for this print:

Happy are those who, born from the red ground,
Do not allow themselves to be disturbed by mirror images of gray,
But continue to ride on gallantly.
Only the horse shyly pulls back its ears
As it glides past yet another.

The endless band of horsemen
Changes from inside to out,
But gray remains gray.
We ride eternally toward and past each other,
Each red one determining a gray other;
But no one is in disarray.

Where the inside curves into the outside,
There is chaste jostling; the ranks close.
We ride silently
To where our mirror image stands waiting,
There I dissolve in my brother's background,
As Escher wills it!

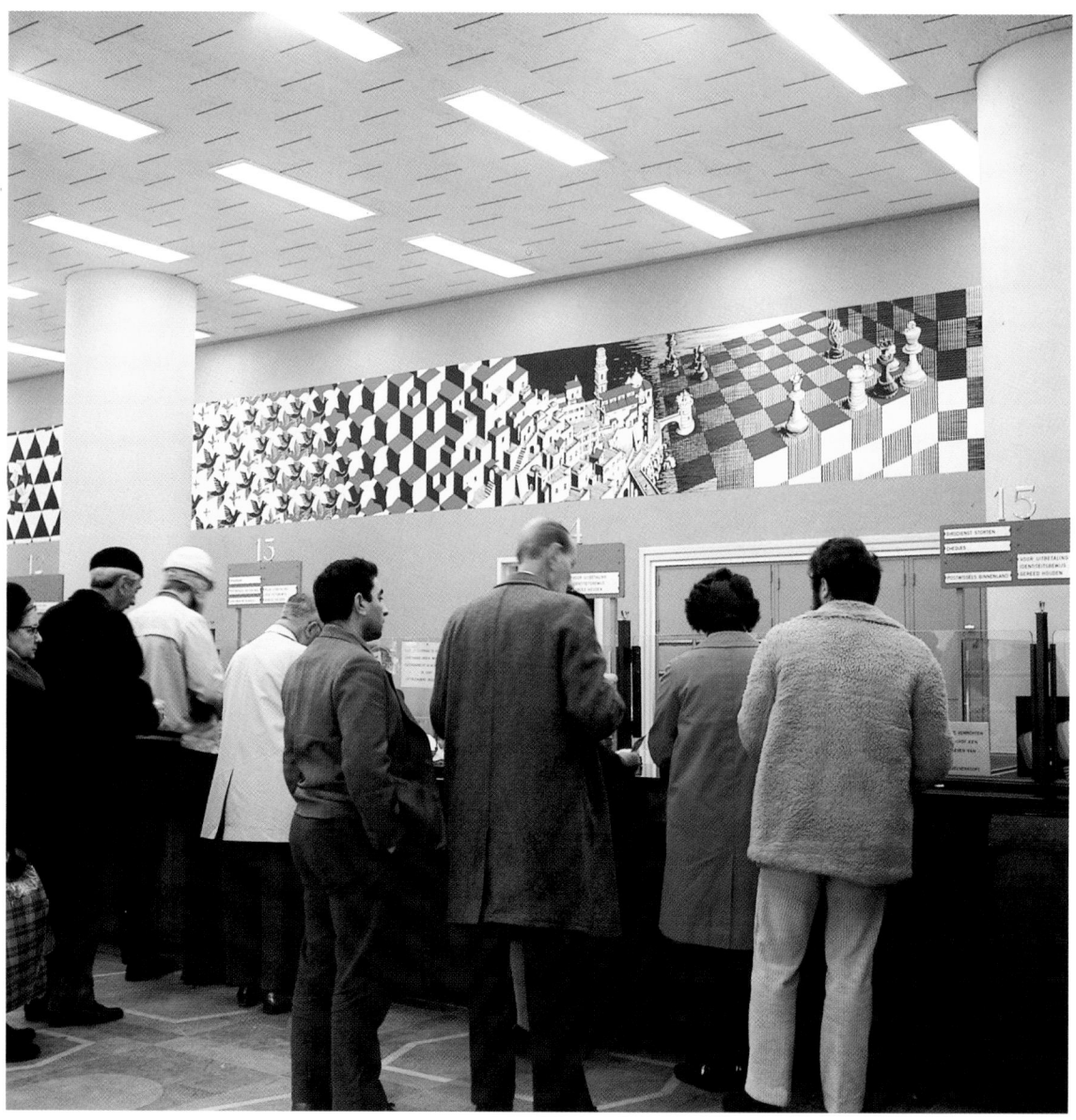

Large Metamorphosis III
Mural a in post office in The Hague, 1968

In 1967, the Dutch Postal Services asked Escher to do a mural with a length of 157 feet for the window service area of a new post office in The Hague. The intention was to have **Metamorphosis** (see page 16) Escher did in 1940 enlarged. It turned out that if this were done, an area of 52 feet of wall space would remain unused. Escher wrote his sons: "[I will have to] add or insert another six and a half feet of new metamorphoses to the original scale of the band of images in the woodcut. It should be possible, but it will be quite a task."

In a letter written in 1968, he said: "I was recently again at the post office in The Hague. They have made very little progress so far, but the young assistant painter (twenty-one years old) is doing a great job and enjoying it very much. It will probably be another six months before the work is completely finished."

1

★

2

★

3

★

4

★

5

★

6

★

7

★

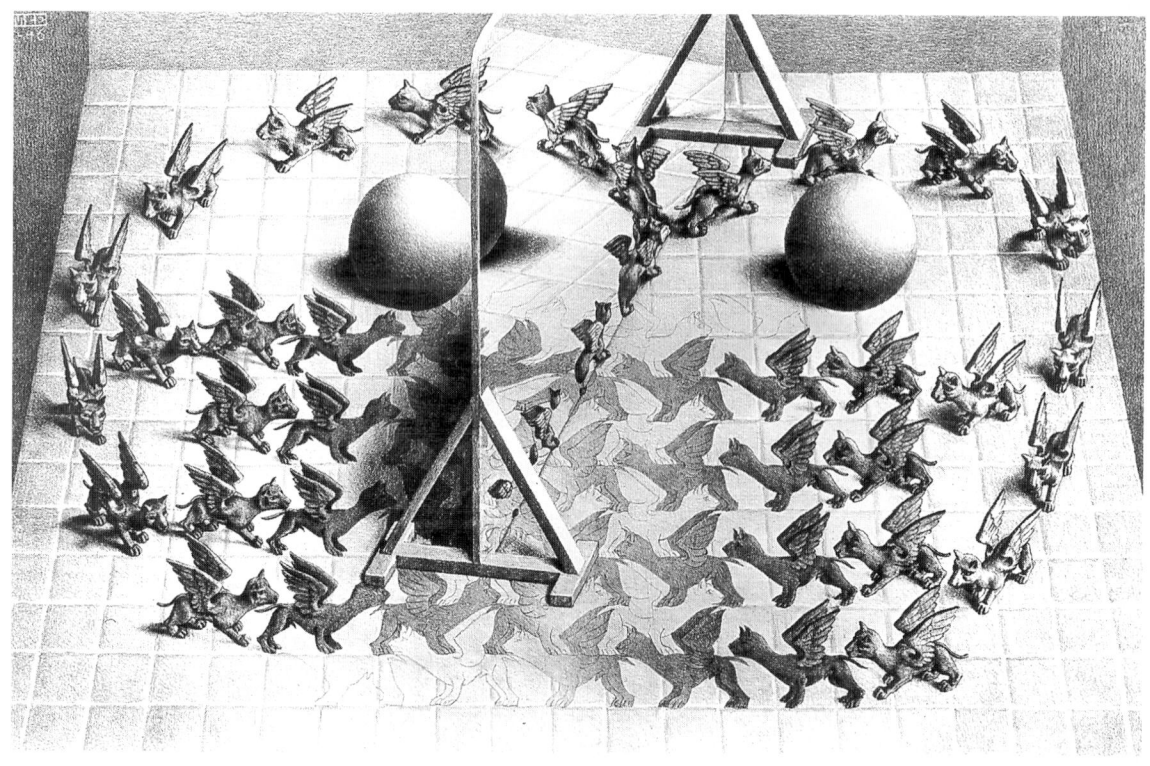

Magic Mirror
Lithograph, 1946

The lithograph **Magic Mirror**, produced in 1946, poses two questions: first, what is the difference between reality and mirror images, and second, how is it possible that we interpret a two-dimensional drawing as three-dimensional reality? The story begins in the lower left-hand corner of the mirror itself, where the tip of a wing protrudes from the mirror. Moving along the surface of the mirror, it gradually becomes a winged dog who, toward the edge of the mirror, walks around to the right. At the same time, its mirror image walks off to the left. The dogs then begin to multiply until they become rows of four. But as they approach the mirror, they appear gradually to lose their three-dimensionality and turn into periodic patterns.

Were they indeed real? And was it a mirror image that circled around to the left? Escher does not give us an answer to this question; all we get is a hint, which remains incomprehensible. To the right, we see a sphere, and to the left, we notice its mirror image. At least we think we do—but maybe we don't.

8   ★

9   ★

10   ★

11   ★

12   ★

13   ★

14   ★

September

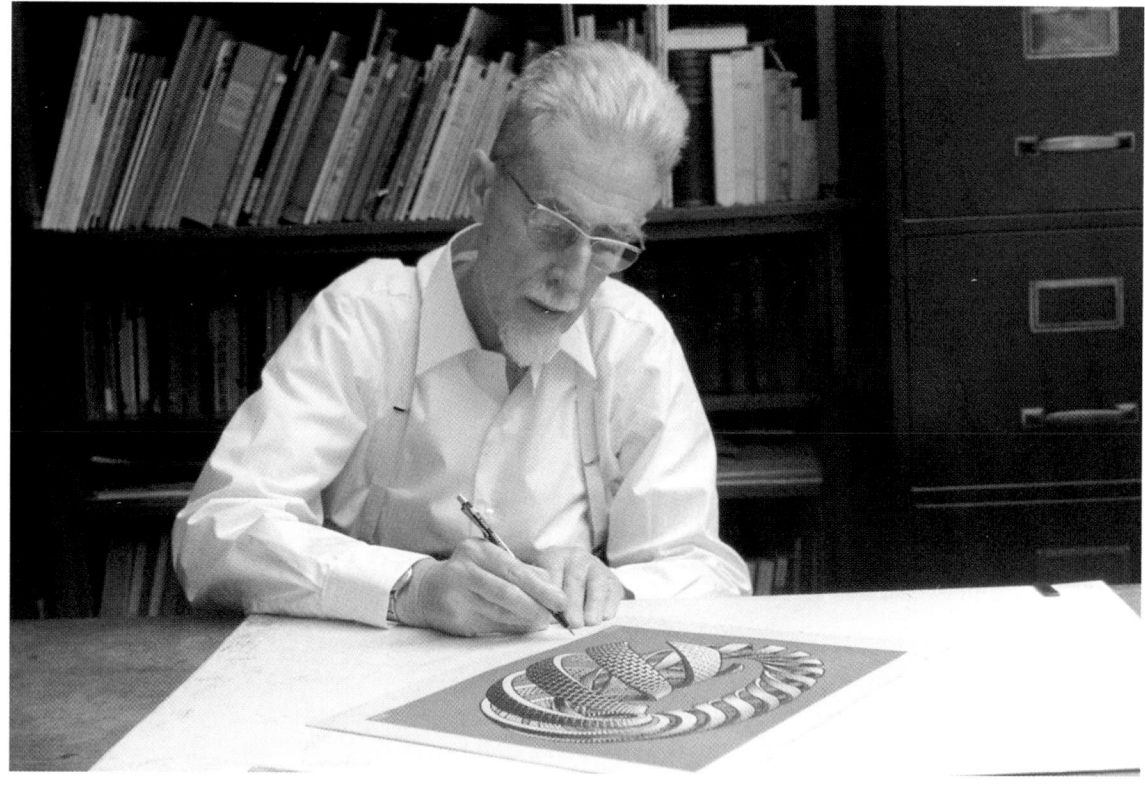

**Escher Signing the Colored
Woodcut Spirals** (*1970*)

In 1969, the last year that Escher
lived in Baarn, I proposed to him
that we record in a book how he
began to develop his artistic
output. "Once you are no longer
with us [death was an ordinary
subject of conversation], people
will find all kinds of mysterious
reasons for it" was how I put it to
him.

Escher thought it was a good
idea, and during the last few years
of his life, I visited him every
Sunday to gather information. I
would then type it up and send it
to him so he could correct it.
"Enclosed are the two pages
describing spirals you sent me. The
material is very clearly presented
and really thoughtful because,
until now, it had never been
researched and described this way

by anyone." On my visit the next
Sunday Escher presented me with
that woodcut and signed it for me.
(Letter 4x, 1970).

15

$\star$

16

$\star$

17

$\star$

18

$\star$

19

$\star$

20

$\star$

21

$\star$

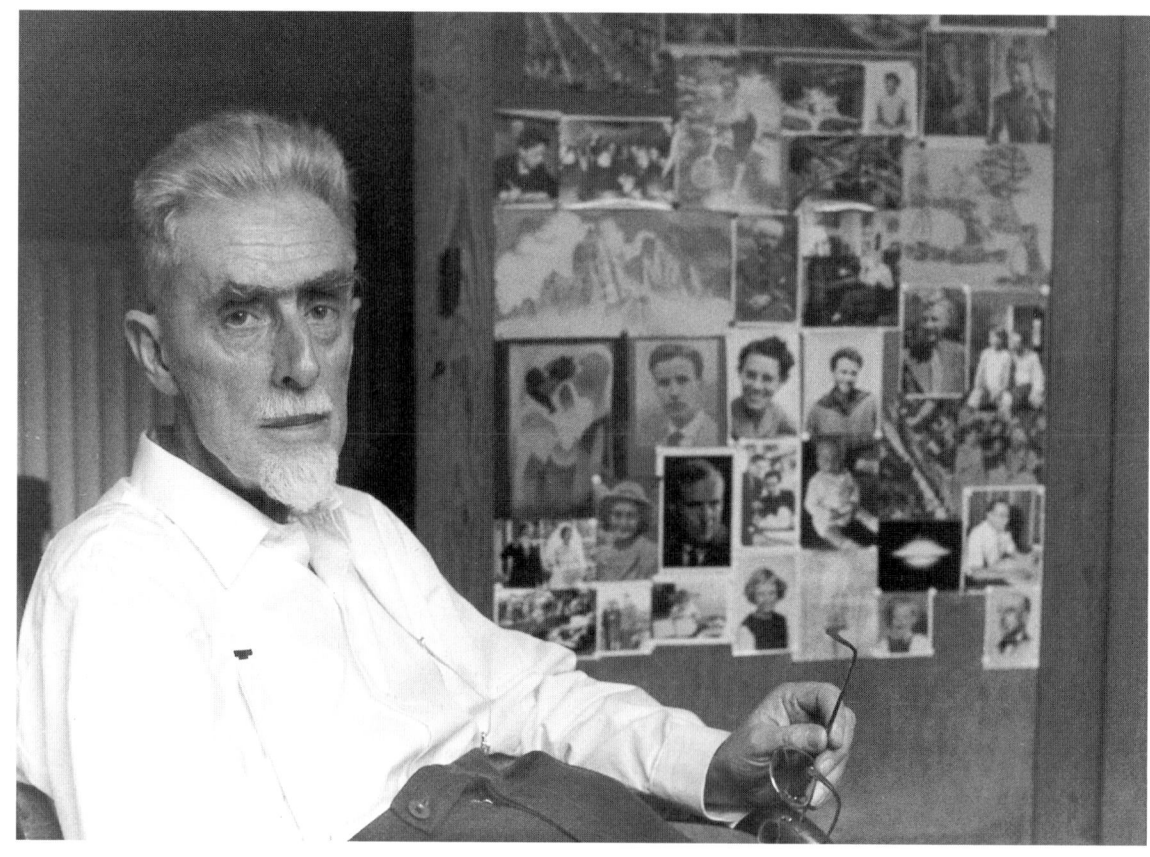

Escher Beside His Tool Closet
(*1969*)

This photograph was taken in 1969, when Escher was working more or less in secret on his last print, **Snakes**. Next to him we see the tool closet, in unfinished wood, where he kept his drawing tools. Escher was attached to this ugly but practical piece of furniture. In fact, in 1970 he took it along to the Rosa Spier Home.

The collection of photographs on the outside of the closet door eloquently attests to several facets of Escher's personality. There are photographs of old friends; of Jessurun de Mesquita; of his wife, children and grandchildren. There are drawings done by his wife and children. But there is also a photograph of Anne Frank that was cut from a newspaper and a postcard, showing an extragalactic system, on which I had sent him a short message.

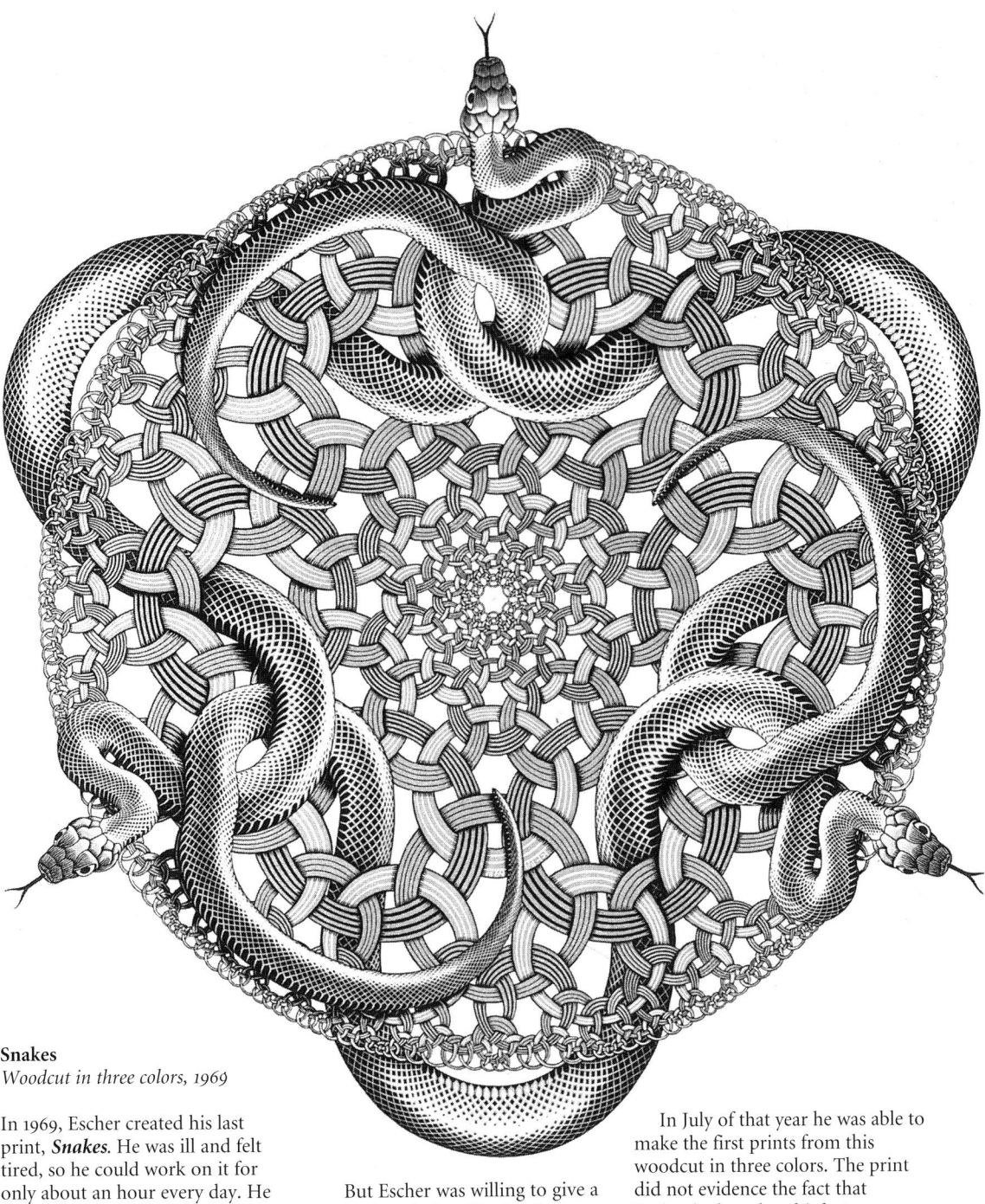

Snakes
Woodcut in three colors, 1969

In 1969, Escher created his last print, **Snakes**. He was ill and felt tired, so he could work on it for only about an hour every day. He did not want to show me his preliminary sketches and stated: "I would not be able to endure it if I saw even a trace of criticism in your eyes. It would take away my courage to continue with it."

But Escher was willing to give a vague description: "A circular coat of mail with small rings along the edges and also in the center of the circle, while the rings in between are larger in size. Snakes would be coiling through the largest rings."

In July of that year he was able to make the first prints from this woodcut in three colors. The print did not evidence the fact that Escher had used up his last reserves in producing it. Everything in this print is muscular and strong; it shows no trace of weariness, illness or old age.

22 ⋆

23 ⋆

24 ⋆

25 ⋆

26 ⋆

27 ⋆

28 ⋆

★

★

September

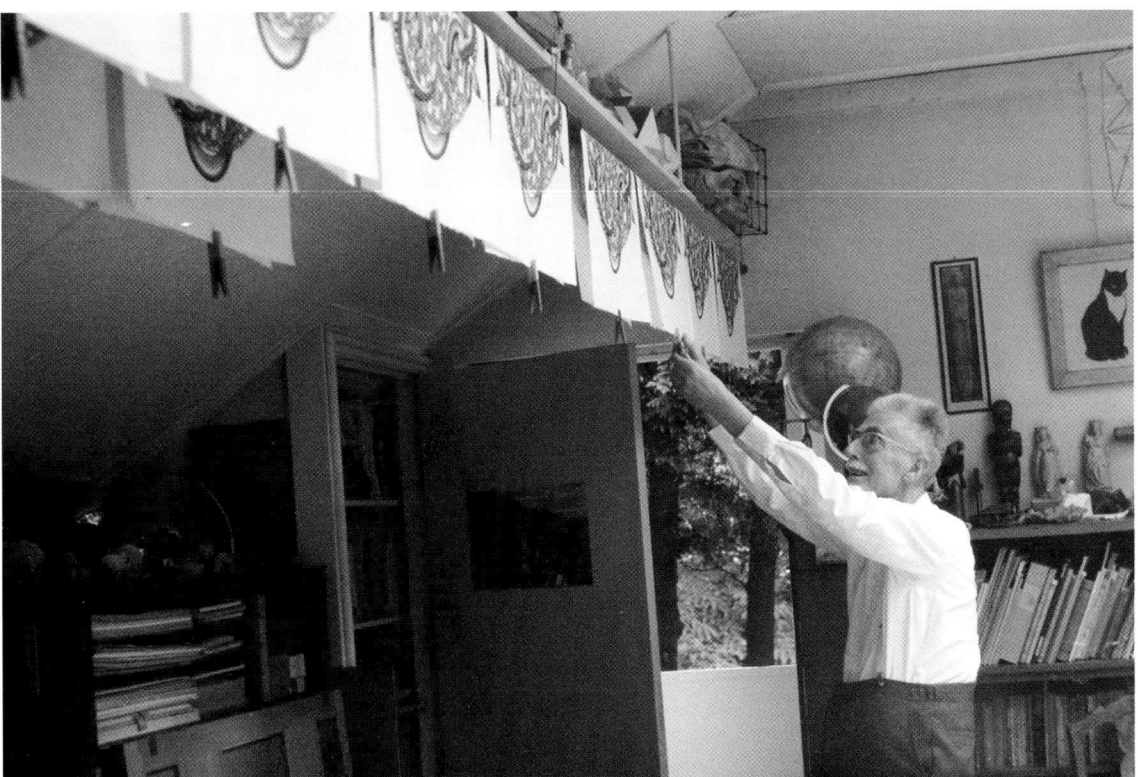

Escher in His Studio in Baarn
(*1969*)

Producing prints from *Snakes* required much time and effort. During one of my visits, Escher proudly showed me twelve prints hanging to dry on a line in his studio. He felt a little better again, and he was also taking part in the making of a film, commissioned by the Ministry of Foreign Affairs, about himself and his work. For a number of his prints, the film used animation to show scenes such as the ascending and descending of the small figures on the staircase without end. Escher enjoyed this very much. The film's value as a documentary was evident, especially in the part where Escher himself talked about his work and in his demonstration of how he produced his woodcuts. This film, originally made to promote Holland, was later shown numerous times as an introduction to lectures about Escher's work.

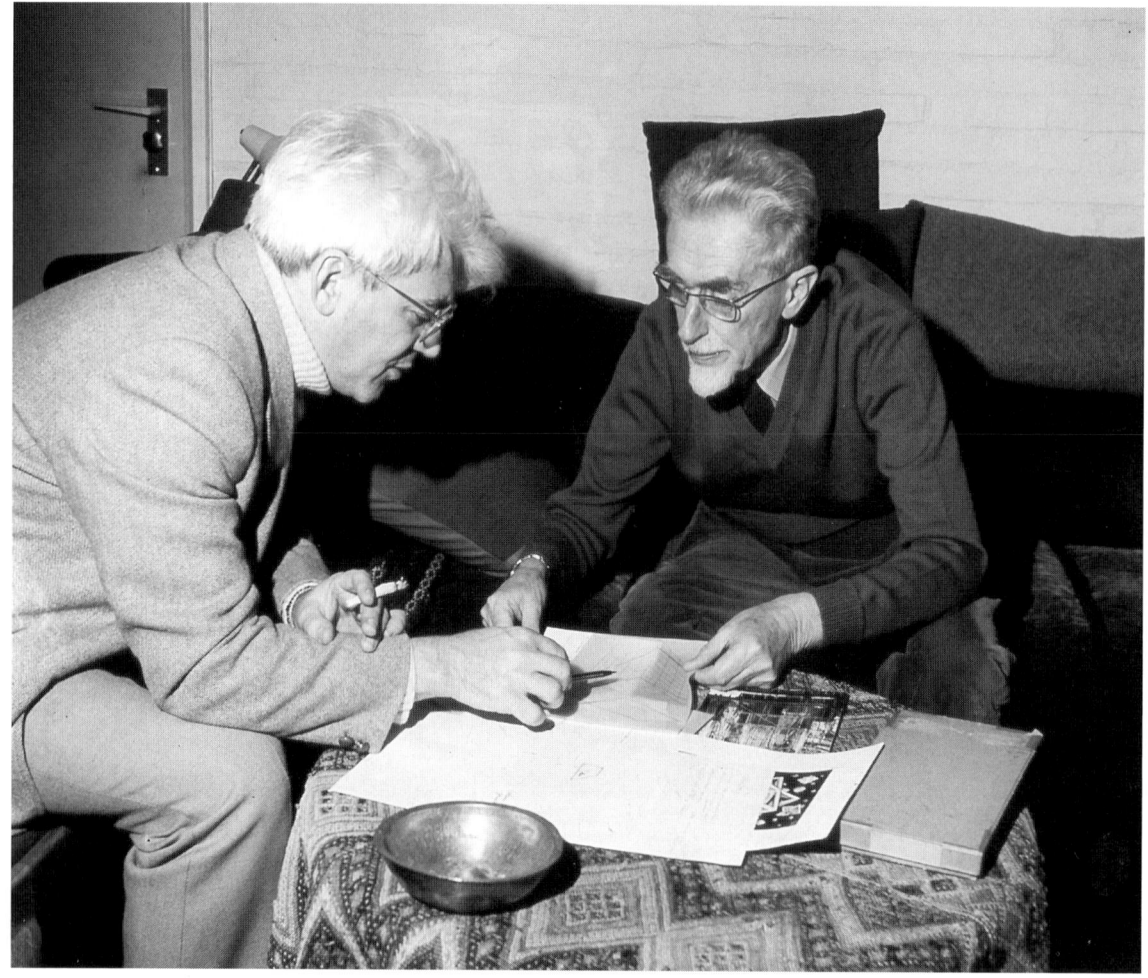

Discussions about *De Toverspiegel* (The Magic Mirror)

The stream of orders for Escher's prints continued to increase steadily, and the prices climbed to figures that seemed incomprehensible to Escher. One Sunday, I expressed amazement about the enormous pile of cardboard rolls in the corridor. With a somewhat melancholy air, Escher said: "The designs I did in 1950 for bank notes were never produced, but now I print them myself in notes of 1000 guilders and higher."

Escher's wife, Jetta, had moved permanently to Switzerland in 1968, and Mrs. Taets van Amerongen had taken over the task of keeping house for him. But his health was failing, and in the spring of 1970 he was hospitalized. From there he wrote me: "I have been in this hospital since March 5th (six weeks already!) and I have had surgery on the large intestine for the fifth time."

After his discharge from the hospital, Escher decided to move into the Rosa Spier Home, a nursing home for elderly artists, in the town of Laren. There he was given a spacious studio next to a living room and, across from these, a separate bedroom. The photograph on this page was taken in the studio during a discussion between Escher and the author.

1

★

2

★

3

★

4

★

5

★

6

★

7

★

8   ⋆

9   ⋆

10   ⋆

11   ⋆

12   ⋆

13   ⋆

14   ⋆

October

15 ★

16 ★

17 ★

18 ★

19 ★

20 ★

21 ★

22 ★

23 ★

24 ★

25 ★

26 ★

27 ★

28 ★

★

★

.

★

Last Photograph Taken of Escher

This is the last photograph I took of Escher in his studio in the Rosa Spier Home. Despite the increasing discomfort he suffered as a result of his illness, he continued to be interested in just about everything. He insisted on making his bed himself, even if it took him hours. After a fifteen-minute walk, he would be exhausted. Sometimes he would end a letter with a complaint: "But what if I am doomed to muddle through the rest of my days like this?" or "I hope so much that I will be around to see the publication of your book; sometimes when I feel so terrible, I fear the worst."

The end came on March 27, 1972. George, Arthur and Jan had arrived in Hilversum around the fifteenth of March. They took turns staying with their father as he lay dying. George described his father's last days to me. His letter ended as follows: "On the 27th, I spent the morning with him as usual. We talked a bit from time to time, and he made a joke about the ridiculousness of his situation that had me chuckling for quite a while. When I walked into the hospital after lunch, Doctor Glazenburg told me that Father had died in the early afternoon."

October

1

                                                        ★

2

    ★

3

    ★

4

    ★

5

    ★

6

    ★

7

    ★

8
          ★

9
          ★

10
          ★

11
          ★

12
          ★

13
          ★

14
          ★

November

15   ★

16   ★

17   ★

18   ★

19   ★

20   ★

21   ★

November

22 ★

23 ★

24 ★

25 ★

26 ★

27 ★

28 ★

29   ★

30   ★

★

★

★

★

1

                                              ★

2

                                              ★

3

                                              ★

4

                                              ★

5

                                              ★

6

                                              ★

7

                                              ★

December

8   ⋆

9   ⋆

10   ⋆

11   ⋆

12   ⋆

13   ⋆

14   ⋆

December

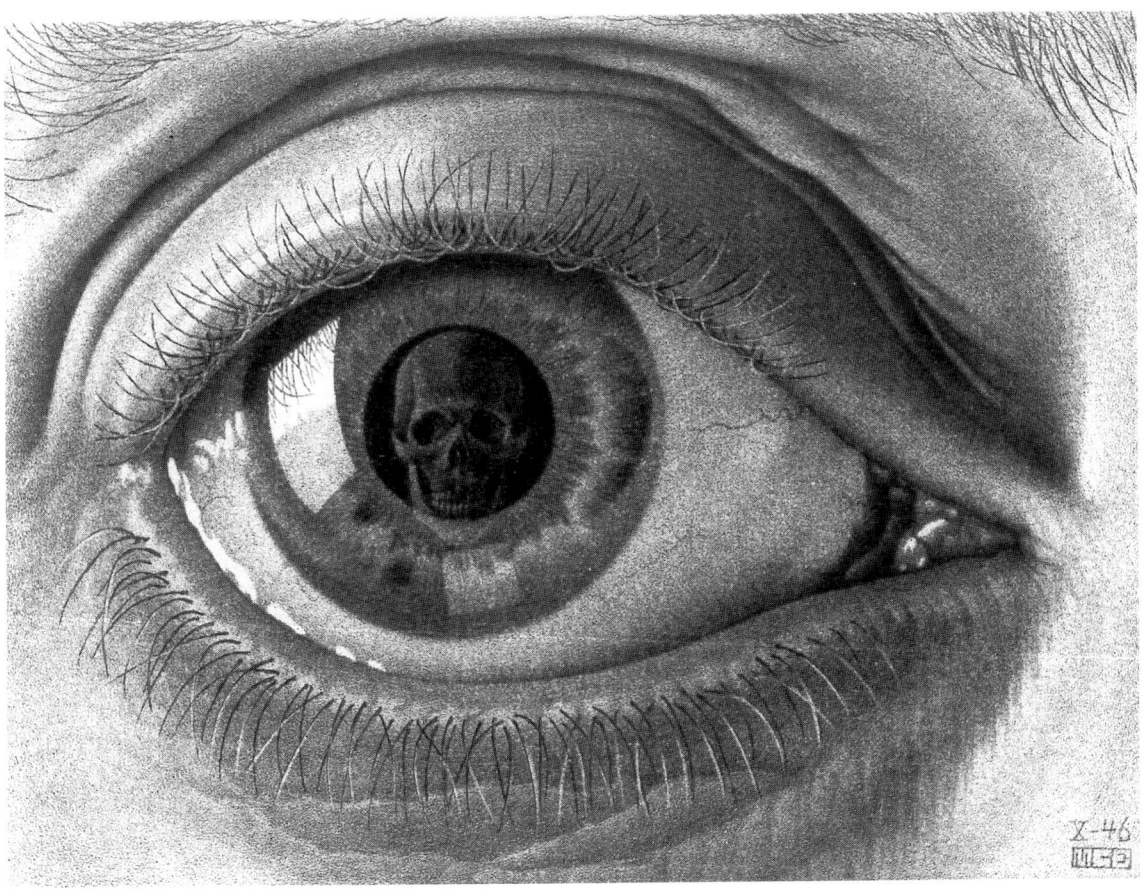

Eye
Mezzotint, 1946

The considerable influence Escher's work has had on the public at large may not be overlooked. Thanks to the millions of reproductions that have been distributed through books and in the form of posters, a great many people have become acquainted with his work. His work not only has evoked amazement (which is important in and of itself) but also has made people aware that *seeing* is a true miracle. When we view one of Escher's prints, our eyes open up as if to see new worlds, which we create in our brains by way of the images on our retinas. The process actually takes place in exactly the same manner as when we look at ordinary things around us. But the result is different, and this element of difference can perhaps best be described as more amazing and more unusual than our daily experiences.

15   ★

16   ★

17   ★

18   ★

19   ★

20   ★

21   ★

22 ⋆

23 ⋆

24 ⋆

25 ⋆

26 ⋆

27 ⋆

28 ⋆

December

119

December

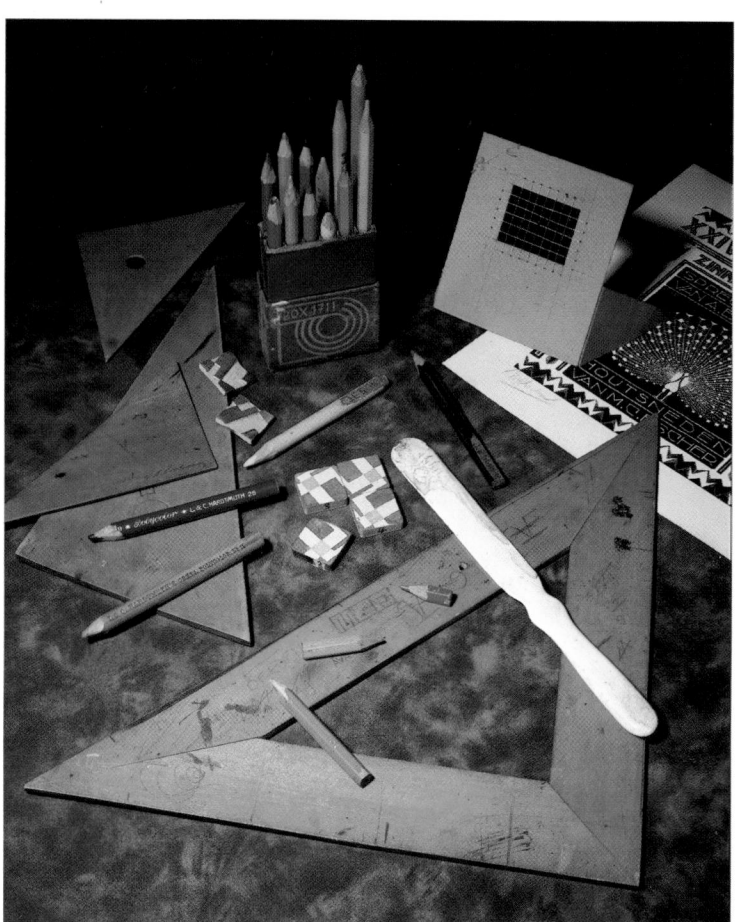

Escher Memorabilia
Photograph by J. Price

These are some small tools Escher used for his work. There are the frugally sharpened colored pencils . . . why did he use so much red? Was this small pencil stump used to color in the periodic patterns? There are the small lino stamps, meticulously cut out, and the much-used triangle with its characteristic initials, MCE. How many lines did he carefully draw along its sides? There is the paper cutter and the lattice of little squares made of sewing thread. All these poignant reminders are silent witnesses of the work of Escher's mind, eyes and hands. A touching scene.